Sex and the New Morality

Sex and the

New Morality

By Frederic C. Wood Jr.

Association Press – New York

Newman Press – New York
Glen Rock, N.J.

SEX AND THE NEW MORALITY

For
Jennifer, Elizabeth, and Barbara

preface

THIS BOOK HAS a strange history. That history may say something cogent about its topic.

In October of 1964, I preached a sermon on sex and morality at Goucher College in Baltimore, Maryland, where I then served as Chaplain. Virtually the same sermon had been preached the year before at Cornell University, where it occasioned no publicity or public response. At Goucher, the response on campus was not unlike that at Cornell — mild interest for a few days and some comment in the college newspaper. However, the response and publicity in the wider Baltimore community was such as to lead quickly to national publicity and a virtual *cause célèbre* for the college and myself.

The result was (1) untold numbers of letters to the President of the college, protesting or supporting my views; (2) more than six hundred letters to me personally from places as far removed as Tokyo and Berlin; (3) considerable agitation within the Goucher Board of Trustees for my dismissal; (4) an open letter from the President to alumnae and parents supporting me personally while taking issue with my views; (5) a public statement by my Bishop to the same effect; and (6) a deluge of invitations for personal speaking and writing. I found myself attacked as everything from anti-American to perverted, and heralded as everything from a prophet to some kind of emancipator. Ironically, I saw myself in none of those roles.

Since I considered my views on this subject to be neither original nor particularly shocking, all of this came as some surprise to me. The only explanation seemed to be that I had touched on more of a raw nerve than I had anticipated. Subsequent experience has borne out this impression. As I have spoken publicly on this topic, discussed it with groups of all ages, explored the available literature, and counseled with individuals, it has been borne in on me that our society is the victim of tremendous confusion in the realms of sex and sexual morality. It is this confusion which I think underlay the panic and irrationality of the Goucher incident of 1964.

I do not suppose that this book will dispel that confusion. I certainly hope it will not add to it. But I do hope that it may aid some in the process of becoming fuller sexual beings and responsible sexual decision-makers.

I am gratified that publishing arrangements have been made to bring this book to the attention of a wider audience of Roman Catholic readers as a contribution to the current Catholic debate on the formation of conscience. This is, of course, also a serious issue for non-Catholics and all whose faith assumes some institutional form. I am hopeful that this book will contribute not only to this debate, but also to the growing Protestant-Catholic-Jewish dialogue on issues which vitally concern all of us.

Thanks are due to my wife and children for patience in the face of my own legalism about my time during two summer vacations; to my research assistant, Miss Nancy Spencer, for typing, proofreading, and making valuable suggestions; and to Mr. Robert Elfers of Association Press for gracious and helpful editorial assistance.

F. C. W. Jr.
Poughkeepsie, New York
January 1968

contents

Introduction 11

1. The Mystery of Sexuality 17
    Sexual Differentiation and Humanness 18
    Sex and Human Relationships 24
    Sexuality and Identity 29
    Attitudes Toward the Body 33

2. The Exploitation of Sexuality: Sexual Immorality . . . 41
    Sex and the Marketplace 43
    The Double Standard 48
    The Cult of the Virgin 53
    Sex and Race 58
    Sex and Violence 60
    Conclusion: The Misuse of the Body 63

3. The Realization of Sexuality: Sexual Morality 65
    Old and New Moralities 66
        The Letter Versus the Spirit 68
        Internal Versus External Loci of Evaluation . . . 73
        Freedom and Responsibility 77
        Morality and Belief 81
    The Ethics of Love 82
    An Optimistic Doctrine of Man 92
    Conclusion: Guidelines? 97

4. Sex and Marriage 99
    Marriage as Covenant 101
        Mutual Consent 102
        Public Assent 104
        Lifelong Intention 108

Sex Within the Covenant 110
  Adultery 111
  Unconventional Forms 113
Sex Outside the Covenant 114
  Three General Questions 116
Sex and Marriage: A Reappraisal 120

5. Beyond Conventional Heterosexuality 123
  Abstinence 124
  Masturbation 129
  Homosexuality 134
  Two Related Issues: Abortion and the Use of Drugs . 140
  Abortion 140
  Sex and Drugs 145

Postscript: Toward an Uncertain Future 149

Notes 151

introduction

IN AN AGE which is sex-saturated and profit-oriented, an author publishing on the topic of sex should begin by examining his motives. This is particularly true where the sex and the profit motifs are frequently combined. Sex sells big in our society. It sells especially big in the field of publications. Consequently, sex is the topic on which it is probably easiest to say less and sell more in print. This is because a sex-saturated society is also a sex-starved society. And these two phenomena are closely related. Our society is starved for real sexual involvement partly because it is so saturated with superficial, phoney, vicarious sex. And in his starvation, contemporary man grasps at more and more sexual superficiality, like a thirst-crazed man drinking salt water.

Does such an age need another addition to its abundant sex literature, and that by a college chaplain? Indeed, the author's profession could be argued as a point against undertaking the present work. This is partly because some will no doubt misinterpret his opinions and illustrations as a reflection of the institution which he serves. Out of prurient delight, they will fail to recognize that opinions can not constitute institutional policies and that illustrations and data reflect widespread trends, and are not limited to any particular campus.

There is, however, a deeper reason for a college chaplain to approach this topic with caution. A popular assumption in our time is that sex is somehow a *special* problem on our college campuses.[1] The hidden agenda here is the misconception that sexual morality is only a dilemma for people who aren't married. In a time when we should know better from the data of divorce statistics and various clinical studies,[2] we persist in the belief that the moral dilemma of sexuality is dissolved by tying the marriage knot. Closely related is the assumption that heterosexual relations represent the only significant moral choice, both before and after marriage. The college chaplain who undertakes to write on sexual morality should caution

11

his readers against any such circumscriptions of his topic.

Indeed, part of the rationale for the present work is the desire to explode some of the myths which surround the subject of sex, as well as to set sexual morality in perspective as a *human* rather than simply a *student* or *unmarried* dilemma.

This book is also prompted by a desire to exorcise the demons who lie behind the joint symptoms of sex starvation and sex saturation in our time. No one should imagine that he can slay these demons single-handedly, let alone with only the printed word. But every effort to set human sexuality in a more natural and realistic perspective, to apply to it an ethic which has to do with more than simply sex, and to counter the illusions propounded by overzealous moralists and profit-hungry opportunists, should be a blow for both sexual freedom and sexual responsibility.

Finally, this book attempts to address the moral dimension of human sexuality from the perspective of that ethical attitude variously labeled the "new morality," "situation ethics," "contextual ethics." There have recently appeared some helpful books discussing human sexuality from a healthy biblical/theological perspective.[3] Most of these touch on the ethical dimensions, but either avoid the "big" ethical questions or fail to make their own point of view and assumptions clear. At the same time, the new morality has in recent years received clear and extensive treatment in print,[4] in spite of the tendency in the mass media to misrepresent it and to sensationalize its sexual implications. Such treatments of the rationale of this "new" ethic usually address themselves, among other things, to sexual decisions. But there has yet to appear a study devoted to sexuality explicitly from the new morality perspective. That is the intention of the present volume.

A brief elaboration of this moral attitude may be helpful here, although a fuller treatment is offered in Chapter 3. The new morality is neither a new moral code nor a more liberal revision of an old code. Indeed, the new morality is not a code at all. It does not prescribe the form and detail of what to do in given situations. It is instead what might best be called an ethical attitude. It is an approach toward the way in which to make decisions most responsibly. It is an attitude toward moral codes and how they are to be applied and related to. It is that moral attitude which searches out the rationale or spirit of any code, and then calls for loyalty to this spirit above loyalty to the letter of particular prescriptions. As such, the new morality encourages (literally, "gives the courage for") both moral freedom and moral responsibility. It encourages moral freedom because it reminds the individual that he finally makes his own decisions. They are not made in advance for him, even by time-tested and sanctified codes. The new morality encourages moral responsibility because it holds up an ideal value (Love) on the basis of which the individual is called to make his decisions. One of the central insights of the new morality is this paradox of moral freedom and responsibility. The two go together. You cannot have one without the other. And just as the encouragement of one means the encouragement of the other, so the inhibition of the one means the inhibition of the other. One of the indictments which the new morality brings against some traditional morality is that in the name of encouraging moral responsibility it has actually inhibited moral freedom and moral responsibility.

It should be clear then that the author resists the equation of sexuality with morality. This needs to be emphasized because of a popular tendency to identify the two, as if the only real moral questions were in the sexual realm and as if the primary significance of sex were its moral dimension. This is reflected in the popular phrase *morals charge,* referring to an alleged sexual offense against the law. Likewise, when one announces that he is going to speak about morality, it is usually assumed that he is going to talk about sex. Such assumptions restrict the concept of morality, which is properly understood as referring to all decision-making. They also contribute to a view of sexuality as the focus of some kind of special moral dilemma. Such thinking is a symptom of the sickness which it perpetuates, like pus which reinfects its own wound.

The approach of this book to its topic is not only moral, but also clinical. It has its roots as much in the author's experience with people in need of counseling help as in any desire to set forth broad principles of right and wrong, healthy and unhealthy, fulfilling and constricting behavior. Indeed, the author's professional training is not in the realm of what is usually called "moral theology." It is rather in the pastoral field. This book arises out of a pastoral ministry which deals with human perplexity in the face of a reality which has the power both to destroy and to fulfill life. Among other things, it is hoped that what follows may contribute to an appreciation of the extent to which the traditional concerns of pastoral theology and moral theology overlap. Relevant ethical theories are grounded in the agonizing perplexities of decision-making of real people as they strive for some kind of human fulfillment, some form of abundant life. Morality, with its related questions of value, meaning, and the nature of right and wrong, is a basic dimension of almost every counseling situation. The roots of the opinions which follow lie not so much in books and logic as in long hours of listening—to a student concerned with premarital behavior, to another with homosexual leanings, to a couple facing an unmarried pregnancy, to a frustrated and unhappy married man, to a wife who feels sexually used by her husband, to a divorcee reflecting on her own unique sexual image and problems.

The "pastoral psychology" movement in theological education in the last four decades provided a needed corrective to preoccupations with the moral dimension of pastoral counseling. But insofar as this has led to a divorcing of ethics from counseling and a preoccupation with therapy, it has erred on the other side. It has also weakened the therapy which it desires, whenever the ultimate values and meaning which a man sees in his life are not viewed as central to his healing.[5] One of the frontiers at which clinical and moral concerns meet is that of sex. Any attempt to deal with the topic must see both dimensions. Otherwise, it will fall into either a functional reductionism which mistakes the symptoms for the substance of health or irrelevant theorizing which mistakes abstract logic for concrete reality.

With such concerns in mind, the present work addresses itself first to the mystery of sexuality in an attempt to define the nature of our central focus. Then we shall examine in order the exploitation and the realization of sexuality, representing respectively sexual immorality and sexual morality. A discussion of the relationship between sex and marriage follows, and then a treatment of forms of sexual self-expression other than the conventionally heterosexual.

It remains to suggest the audience to whom this book is addressed. One is tempted to answer: to all for whom their sexuality is experienced as a self-conscious realm for moral decisions. That is in a sense accurate. And I would hope that what is offered here will be found relevant by all who are aware of their sexuality and have a sense of moral responsibility in regard to it. At the same time, I have particularly in mind a somewhat narrower audience. That audience consists primarily of those with whom I have over the past several years counseled as they struggled with both the power and the mystery of their own sexuality. One sees them in all kinds of dilemmas, moral and otherwise. One is trying to decide whether or not to sleep with her boyfriend. Another is trying to come to grips with her feelings toward her roommate who does. One is trying to decide why he masturbates, another why it bothers him, and a third how he can stop. One is trying to pull herself together after an unsuccessful "affair," while another is deciding whether to have an abortion or marry him. And some are much less dramatic, like the young man who wants to understand why he is frightened by women, or the young woman who has unacceptable thoughts when she looks at a man.

These are for the most part young, unmarried people. Although their decisions are not always in the heterosexual realm, they usually are. They are those who are most clearly the victims of our society's confusion, hypocrisy, and sickness in the realms of sexuality and sexual morality. This does not undercut what I have said earlier concerning sex as a moral domain for all people, young and old, married and unmarried. It is simply an acknowledgement that the young (who are usually the unmarried) are the most obvious and in some ways the most salvageable victims of any society's sicknesses.

1

the mystery
of sexuality

ONE OF THE MOST OBVIOUS facts of human existence is one which man apparently finds it hardest to accept. It is the fact of his sexuality. Man is inescapably and irreducibly a sexual creature. No matter what kind of cross-sectional view he takes of himself, no matter from what perspective he strives to understand himself, man is always confronted with the fact of his own sexual differentiation. That this differentiation is a basic mark of human existence is as true of theological views of man as it is of psychological, sociological, anthropological, and physiological views. Sexuality is as basic to man's life in the world as is the fact that he walks in an upright position and has a highly developed brain.

If sexuality is so obvious and basic, why is it also such a mystery? Why has sexuality traditionally been an object of awe, reverence, fear, and fascination? Probably because man from primitive times has sensed that within his sexuality there lies *power*. This is not simply the power of reproduction, although the relationship between sex and reproduction is fundamental to man's awe in the face of his sexuality. But sexuality—with its needs, drives, and promises—also has the power to inspire great and foul deeds, to determine the decisions men make, and to alter the course of history. Therefore, sexuality is the object of both adoration and fear. Man senses the promise which it holds. He also senses its dangerous power over him. He senses its power to destroy as well as to build up.[1] He senses how basic sexuality is to his deepest and most mysterious emotions. He senses how basic it is to the experience of love . . . but also to the experience of hate.

Is it possible to undo this mystery? Would it be helpful to resolve this mystery and learn to treat the fact of our sexuality much as we treat the fact of a digestive system and other organic functions? No. It is not possible to remove this mystery. Furthermore, even if it were possible, it would not be advisable. It is not possible because to remove the mystery of sexuality man would have to remove its power, both psychological and physiological. Without the promise, threat, and spur of that power, man would probably become an altogether different creature. Also, the undoing of the mystery of sexuality might transfer its power to another base, where it might be more readily exploited.

From time to time, of course, man has attempted either to remove or to ignore the mystery of his sexuality. A misunderstanding and misuse of some of the insights of Sigmund Freud leads to the former error. A misunderstanding and misuse of the institutions of monasticism and celibacy leads in the latter direction. Where sexuality is de-mystified, the power of one man's sexuality can fall into another man's hands, as in some abortive psychotherapy[2] and in the attempt of the state to reduce and control the power of sexuality in George Orwell's *1984*.[3] Where sexuality is ignored, self-conscious responsibility for the power of one's own sexuality is abdicated. And the power simply expresses itself in some new disguise.

The present work is intended neither to remove nor to ignore the mysterious dimension of human sexuality. It is, however, intended to set sexuality in a context where it can be accepted as a fact of life, as a natural and wholesome dimension of being human.

SEXUAL DIFFERENTIATION AND HUMANNESS

Sexual differentiation is basic to our humanness. An important part of any definition of human nature is the fact that we are all either male or female. Indeed, there is a real sense in which we are all complicated mixtures of maleness and femaleness.[4] I do not know, for example, what it really means to be human except as I experience humanness through my personal maleness. And this maleness is in turn defined by its complementary side, femaleness. One experiences and becomes aware of his sexuality in the interaction of human relationships. And the basic model for those relationships is male/female. This is true even when the relationship is between two people of the same sex. It is one of Freud's lasting contributions to human self-understanding to have pointed out just this.[5]

This male/female polarity is basic to the biblical understanding of man, although the biblical frame of reference is consistently patriarchal, and at times aggravates the distinction between male and female as separate beings.[6] But in the priestly creation myth in the first chapter of Genesis it is clear that the nature of the human creature is to be both male and female:

> So God created man in his own image, in the image of
> God he created him; male and female he created them.[7]

According to this view, to be man is to be both male and female. Neither masculinity nor femininity of itself yields an adequate understanding of humanness. They must be grasped in their complementarity to yield a full image of man. In other words, the nature of man is revealed in the tension between his maleness and his femaleness. This particular biblical writer also suggests that the nature of man reveals something about the nature (image) of ultimate reality as man experiences it. This is a bold assertion that sexuality inheres in the godhead, that man's experience of the reality he calls God includes maleness and femaleness. If human personhood points to the personal nature of the biblical God/spirit, then the sexual differentiation of human personhood says something important about man's experience of this God. This is consistent with the New Testament affirmation that God is Love,[8] since Love is only given content by the dynamic interaction of human beings. And the basic, definitive mode of that interaction is male/female. This insight also sheds light on Paul's conviction that in Christ "there is neither male nor female."[9] That is not a rejection of sexuality or a repudiation of the sexual differentiation. It is rather a reaction against the patriarchal ethos of Paul's time, which distorted sexual differentiation into an anti-Love (anti-God) segregation of humanity along sexual lines. Paul is saying that in man's ideal state of at-one-ness with the God/ Spirit who is Love, the sexual differentiation will no longer be a source of alienation, division, exploitation, and injustice among men. The context should make this clear because this differentiation is paralleled to that between slave and free, Jew and Greek. Each represents an unnatural and unloving ordering of humanity.

Recent researches into the chemical composition of the human body point to the same holistic, integrative view of sexuality. Increased awareness of the necessary hormone balance of the human organism has taught us that physiologically we are all quite literally mixtures of maleness and femaleness. Indeed, we have learned that without this balance within each organism we could not survive. And medical science is just now in the process of adjusting this hormone balance to help individuals lead fuller lives.

Carl G. Jung was a pioneer on the same track when he elaborated his concepts of the anima and the animus.[10] These abstractions represent psychological expressions of our femaleness and maleness. Jung was saying that psychologically each of us has a male and a female side. Each of us reacts according to both male and female modes, the dominant mode depending on our sexual identity. Where, for example, the physiological determinants of sexuality are male, the anima (or female spirit) is revealed as exercising an important, although hidden or suppressed, power over the individual.

Jung was not unaware of the metaphysical and theological implications of this insight. He rightly perceived that the godhead itself is perceived and experienced by man in male and female modes.[11] The patriarchal bias of the Judeo-Christian tradition notwithstanding, God is both male and female. The fundamental inner reality (archetype) which man calls God is experienced as "having" both anima and animus, as being both male and female spirit. And from this Jung recognized the rich female imagery of much paganism and the Roman Catholic veneration of Mary as a step toward psychological and theological maturity from the arid male exclusivism of traditional Judaism and Protestantism. Indeed, he identified the enunciation of the dogma of the assumption of the Virgin as (from a psychological view) the most significant event in the history of Christendom since the Reformation!

Why is it important to recognize this role which sexual differentiation plays in our perception of our humanness and of ultimate reality? Because failure to accept it can lead man to illusions about himself which dangerously threaten his realization of his full humanity. At least three of these illusions are easily identifiable in our time. One is the segregation of the human race along sexual lines into higher and lower orders. A second is the focusing of sexual differentiation on genital distinctions and functions. And a third illusion is the tendency to view sexuality as some kind of "extra," tacked on to human nature in two types as an unfortunate necessity.

Dividing humanity into two types of being, male and female, denies man's full humanity under the pretension of sexual self-sufficiency. Thus, the sexual definition of a man (one having male sexual differentiation) is not distinguished from the generic definition of man (one who is human). And the complementary nature of femininity is ignored so that man lives under the illusion that he can be fully human without woman. Such thinking is manifested in most patriarchal societies, is deeply embedded in the medieval world-view,[12] and is still emotionally and politically powerful in an age when many speak of the "emancipation" of women. It lends itself to the illusion of masculine superiority, intellectually and morally as well as physiologically. And it usually leads to the treatment of women as inferior and not entitled to the full rights and privileges of citizenship. In sexual practices it leads to a view of women as things. They are property to be used for the gratification of the male and (conveniently) for the perpetuation of the species. This last dehumanizing of women on sexual grounds led to the assumption which Freud encountered in many of his patients[13] that it was slightly indecent for a woman to enjoy sexual intercourse!

The same division of humanity into two orders leads to a moral double standard, where standards of sexual practice which are binding on women are not binding on men. The double standard not only ignores the fact that it takes two to commit the sexual act; it also leads to a depersonalizing kind of thinking about feminine chastity and virginity. Like most ideological weapons, the sexual double standard ultimately deprives those who exploit it. In western culture it has often deprived the male of a sexual partner who meets him as a true *partner* in an act of genuine self-giving love. This is because his potential partner has been relegated to the realm of "mere" property. In this, the sexual double standard is like the legal double standard applied to Negroes in the southern United States for many years and still practiced where the advocates of white supremacy hold the reins of government. Because the white man in the South had one law for the Negro and another for himself, he effectively deprived himself of the Negro as a human partner in creating a viable legal framework for southern society. He should not therefore be surprised when those whom he views as "outsiders" try to create this framework for him.

Secondly, the failure to accept a holistic view of sexuality leads to a focus on genitality as the only significant dimension of sexual differentiation. This gives rise to what we might call "genital preoccupation." It also leads to various forms of fantasy and magical thinking in regard to genital parts of the body. Genital preoccupation means an unrealistic emphasis on the genital area in sexual practices, in the modes of a man and a woman coming together. It is seen in the assumption that genital orgasm represents sexual "success" for the female as well as the male. A disillusioned young wife reflects on her marital sex life that it is little more than "mutual masturbation."

The other side of this coin is a neglect of the extent to which one's sexuality pervades one's whole being, style, and identity, to say nothing of one's *whole* body. Although everyone knows where the doctor looks first when a new baby is born, sexuality and identity are by no means exhausted by the type of equipment which is evident. Genitalia are important symbols and symptoms of one's sexuality. They are not its only focus. And to make such symbols exhaustive of the reality to which they point is to practice the same kind of idolatry as those who confuse symbols of God with that reality itself.

Because of this identification of genitality with sexuality, much of what passes for sexual intercourse is actually little more than genital contact. It is glorified petting in which the genitals become the exclusive focus of the sexual act, rather than a full meeting of male and female beings who complete one another in their meeting. When this happens, the full humanity of neither partner is realized, and each leaves the encounter feeling both guilty and cheated — guilty for not having fulfilled the other, cheated out of his or her own fulfillment. This is because the dependence of their common humanity on the relationship of male to female was not adequately recognized or acknowledged. Where sexuality is reduced to genitality, sexual fulfillment is reduced to genital orgasm. A holistic view of sexuality attacks genital preoccupation with the alternative understanding that I, rather than simply my genitals, am all male. And another is *all* female. And neither of us is fully human without the other. Therefore, in order to be fully human, I need another as a person, not simply the occasional use of someone's genitals.

A third illusion views human sexuality as an auxiliary to human existence. Sexuality is a fact, but it is an incidental one, tacked on to human nature for the preservation of the species. This illusion is also dispelled by a holistic view which sees sexuality as part and parcel of human identity.

The view of sexuality as an "extra," which is, like one's thyroid, not essential to human nature but essential to preservation, leads finally to the mechanization of sexuality. This is another form of dehumanization which makes sexuality itself into a thing, detached from an individual's personhood. One's sexuality becomes then a neutral entity, a fact which he must come to grips with, but primarily something to be used or not used as one sees fit. This is closely related to the view which focuses sexuality in the genital area. It is reflected in a statement a clergyman once made to a group of high school girls when he told them that if they did not protect their virginity they would have to face the prospect of presenting themselves to their husbands as "used goods" on their wedding nights!

Such a view makes the heterosexual act of intercourse a mechanical performance, a charade in which two people use certain equipment to achieve certain ends without ever necessarily meeting as people. Worse still, such a view misses the important point that sexuality is essential to humanity — and that a detached or detachable sexuality means a detached or detachable humanity.

Where sexuality is an extra dimension of human nature it can be seen not only as neutral and mechanical, but as debased and demonic. Because the church has traditionally acknowledged the power and mystery of sexuality, it has also from time to time flirted with this latter heresy — the debasing of sexuality. Thus, there is an ascetic tradition in Christianity in which refraining from overt genital involvement is considered more godly, clean, chaste. According to this view, sexuality is not only an extra. It is an unfortunate, although necessary extra. It tempts man away from true communion with his God to a tainted communion with another person in the world. It tempts man away from that which is pure and good and holy.[14] According to this view, sexuality is related to a body which is inferior to the human spirit. And man's sexuality tempts him to defile his body still further through contact with another body. It is one of the ironies of the history of Christian thought that such a view could develop out of a theology which is incarnational. This theology identifies God as a reality encountered in the rough and tumble of life in the world, in relationships among persons, literally "in the flesh."[15]

SEX AND HUMAN RELATIONSHIPS

Sex is also mysterious because it is so basic to all human relationships. This is as true of relationships between members of the same sex as of those between opposite sexes. All our relationships

— parent-child, brother-sister, man-to-man, woman-to-woman — are strongly influenced by our sexuality, and have both implicit and explicit sexual overtones.

It is Freud who made this more clear than anyone else, particularly in his examination of the incest motif in the psychodynamics of family life.[16] The incest motif is basically heterosexual, but it points to phenomena such as the Oedipus complex which have to do with our relationships with members of our own sex. What is true of the most intimate relationships of family life also extends to one's relationships with the broader family of man. There is a sense in which, for example, every relationship with a significantly older man is a reenactment of one's father-relationship, every encounter with a peer provides the occasion for a reenactment of a brother-relationship.

Those who are offended by such insights usually reveal that they have a negative image of their sexuality, and that it has a power over them which they are unwilling to admit. The man who cannot acknowledge sexual overtones in his relationship to his best friend, that he is both attracted to him and competitive with him in ways that have to do with their common sexuality, will also probably be reluctant to acknowledge his dependence on women for the realization of his full humanity. A fear of the sexual dimension of some relationships points to a fear of the sexual dimension of all relationships. Most societies instill an aversion to overt homosexual practices and tend to suppress the sexual dimension of homogeneous relationships. This recognizes the social threat which overt homosexuality poses, that it can become a surrogate for genuine heterosexual fulfillment. And, in this, taboos on overt homosexuality can be appropriate. But insofar as these taboos teach revulsion at the thought of homosexuality, they prevent man from acknowledging the sexual dimension of all his relationships and deprive him of full participation in those relationships. For example, a woman's relationship with her sister or best friend may be enriched by an acceptance of its attractive and competitive sexual overtones without precipitating overt homosexuality. Indeed, such open recognition can deter the con-

striction of sexual expression which overt homosexuality often represents. That overt male homosexuality appears to be more widespread
in our society than homosexuality among females may reflect greater
tolerance of affection and physical contact between women than
between men. Kissing, holding hands, and other forms of sexual
expression between women are widely accepted, even on our sex-
fearing American scene. Ironically, this reflects an essentially masculine assumption that women are less sexually "charged" than men.
They are consequently viewed as less inclined to engage in overt
homosexual union. Homosexuality will be discussed at greater length
in Chapter 5. Our attitudes toward it are cited here as illustrative
of a general unwillingness to accept the sexual dimension of *all,*
rather than simply romantic heterosexual relationships.

The use of the homosexual illustration does not mean that this
is the only form of relationship other than the conventionally heterosexual which has strong sexual overtones. As Freud has pointed out,
we must also learn to accept the sexual dimension of parent-child
relationships, both homosexual and heterosexual. It is unfortunate
in this connection that the Oedipus theory reinforces traditional
biases concerning masculine sexual aggressiveness by positing the
young boy as the aggressor toward his mother. Subsequent theorizing
has tried to point out that the mother is also an aggressor in the
Oedipus syndrome.[17] Likewise, probably the most common incidence
of incest has to do with father-daughter relationships. And it is likely
that the young girl is as aggressive and provocative of this relationship as the father. The brother-sister syndrome is marked by the
same dynamics. A young coed explains her sleeping with her boyfriend with the statement that "he reminds me so much of my brother
that I can't resist him." And further involvement in this case revealed that most of the resistance was on the side of the male, not
the female!

What is being urged here is not an argument for sexual reductionism, a charge which Jung somewhat unjustly leveled at Freud.[18]
Sexual reductionism traces all interpersonal phenomena to a sexual

basis. It is a way of saying that any interpersonal relationship or act is "nothing but" an expression of a sexual drive. It is best illustrated by the response of one psychoanalyst to accounts of heroism by American GI's in rescuing wounded comrades under fire in the Korean War: "Nothing but repressed homosexuality." Such reductionism makes the error of ignoring the complexity of motivational factors which go into any decision, any relationship. It may well be that there is a sexual dimension to the unconscious motives which cause one man to risk his life for another. But to reduce those motives to one dimension is as absurd as reducing one's enjoyment of fishing to his taste for fish. There are multiple factors operative in the dynamics of any human relationship. What is being argued is that one of those factors is inevitably sexual. One factor is the expression of the sexuality of the parties to the relationship. Sex is fundamental to all human relationships.

This does not mean that overt sexual expression is a necessary aspect of all human relationships. The sexual dimension of a relationship may express itself in various forms. In one's relationship with a professional colleague, for example, it may express itself in tennis matches which provide an opportunity for acting out their aggressive competition with one another for sexual partners. Wrestling on the bed with one's six-year-old daughter is not only a healthy expression of mutual affection and enjoyment. It can also be an expression of common sexual attraction. The firm handshake and steady gaze which characterize the greeting of some men denote not only sincerity and integrity, but also personal intercourse sealed in physical contact. This is most obvious in the physical contact and caressing which mark the relationships of most animal lovers with their pets. This is not to suggest that all animal lovers are sodomists at heart. It is simply to point out that the human-animal projection of interpersonal relationships carries with it the sexual overtones of all interpersonal relationships. Any animal lover knows this. Society is more tolerant of this form of overt sexual expression than of many others because it does not seem to be threatening to society itself. It is no accident that many people who live alone tend to establish unusually close and meaningful relationships with their pets.

All of this is important because of the centrality of human relationships to man's life in the world. *Homo sapiens* is irreducibly a social animal. This is fundamentally because of his bisexual nature. But it is also related to evolutionary developments which have made him dependent on his fellow man for his own preservation. No matter how small or large the normative social unit, human life is social life. It always centers on some social unit, be it family, clan, tribe, or nation. In spite of the uncooperative tendencies which mark many of his relationships, man is essentially a cooperative being. Not only is he his brother's keeper, but his brother is his keeper. And they are mutually dependent on one another for their continued life in the world. This is as true economically and politically as it is psychologically and theologically. One of the best hopes for some form of world peace lies in the progressive shrinking of man's world to the point where the economic and political dimensions of social interdependence will become so pressing as to force a *Pax terrestra* on the world.[19] Ironically, when and if this happens, a force to be overcome will be the propensity to violence, which is also an expression of man's sexual aggressiveness and needs.

Because interpersonal relationships are so basic to man's life in the world, it is important to recognize their essentially sexual dimension. Otherwise, man will be less capable of coping creatively with the forces which he finds let loose in them. These forces, including nonviolence as well as violence, the motivation for martyrdom as well as masochism, are expressions of human sexuality and its fundamental power. That human relationships are fundamental to life in the world points us back to the insight that sex is fundamental to life in the world, and not just because it leads to reproduction and the preservation of the species. In a time when man's tendencies toward violence threaten to destroy human life altogether, and when a gospel of Love is loudly proclaimed but rarely heeded as the resolution of the human dilemma, man can afford to ignore the sexual dimension of both violence and love only at his own peril.

SEXUALITY AND IDENTITY

The above discussion points toward a recognition of the relationship between sexuality and identity. *Identity* here refers to a subjective sense of "who" a person is, including perceptions of appropriate social roles, modes of relationship, and styles of life. In this sense, personal identity is quite close to what some psychologists mean by self-image.[20] A person's self-image is the picture he has of himself, his concept of who he is. It is usually revealed in the ways a person describes himself. Frequently it is indicated by what a person thinks others think of him, which can be a projection of his own attitudes toward himself.

This self-image has a form and the form is bodily. Because it is bodily, it is marked by sexual differentiation. And sex is correspondingly basic to one's sense of his own identity, as well as to the identity which he ascribes to others. If you ask me who I am, one of the first things I am going to tell you is that I am either male or female. I may do this by telling you my name, which usually points to sexual identity. I may tell you of one or another social role which I fulfill. For example, I am the husband of so-and-so, or the father of someone else. I may do it by telling you about my vocation or favorite pastimes, which may have strong sexual identifications. For example, the vocation of a truck driver points to one sexual role, that of a nurse to another. A hobby of hunting points to a masculine role in our society, while that of sewing points to a feminine role. And these identifications are embedded in our sense of personal identity. Ponder for a moment the prevailing social reaction to a woman who hunts or a man who sews. Something has confused their identity in our minds. There is something perplexingly inconsistent here. And we consider them "odd," even if we are able intellectually to accept the unorthodoxy of their tastes.

Nowhere is this more clear than in the realm of names. One's name is a clue to and symbol of his identity. The Hebrews forbid the speaking of the name of God because that would be to get too close to God.[21] It would also be potentially idolatrous insofar as the name/symbol might become confused with the reality to which it points. Likewise, in the Christian rite of baptism, the initiate is given a name. This betokens belief that something fundamental has happened to his identity, "who" he is, when he enters the community of faith. Our reaction to men who have names usually associated with femaleness and to women who have what are ordinarily masculine names shows how deeply the relationship between name and identity is ingrained. We tend to be slightly confused or embarrassed by such people. Their identity has been called into question in the deepest reaches of our psyches. And we often react with such comments as: "How cruel of his parents to saddle him with such a name!" What we are really saying is that the sexuality of this person is contradicted by his name. There is something inconsistent between his perceived identity and one of its prime symbols.

Another clue to the relationship between sexuality and identity is our common reaction to the birth of a child. "Is it a boy or a girl?" we ask. And this is generally followed by: "What did you name it?" With the first question we are saying that we cannot come to grips with a new human being's existence until we can identify him sexually. With the second question we are saying that we cannot come to grips with sexuality until we have a symbol or handle for it. Imagine the reaction of most people when parents neglect to name their child for several days after his birth. The child is somehow not yet a full person. We tend to feel that he has been deprived of his identity. And one reason is that he has not been given that outward and visible sign which points to his sexuality.

The same motif underlies the popular fascination of stories in which a man masquerades as a woman or a woman as a man.[22] Part of the attraction of such heroes represents the less dominant side of our own sexuality asserting itself. And the reader is being let in on a monumental secret of which most of the characters in the story are unaware. The reader thus enjoys his superiority over those whose

basic human responses are incongruous. He also vicariously participates in the transformation of identity which attends a switch of
sexual roles.

Our perception of our sexuality is also related to traditional and
socially acceptable sexual roles. This means that our sense of our
own identity and the identity which we ascribe to others is informed
by the roles which we play. This is true, even though the sexual identification of roles is usually culturally conditioned. Americans, for
example, seeing a picture of a Russian woman carrying a gun and a
belt of bullets, assume that Russian women are coarse and masculine. The image presented by the picture conflicts with those roles
which we associate with femaleness. Consequently, the sexual identity of the Russian woman is called into question. Likewise, a French
fashion designer whose hair is slightly longer than the American
norm, whose hands are slender and delicate, and whose bodily movements do not exude the violent aggressiveness we associate with
masculinity, evokes an ambiguous response. There is something con-
fusing about his identity. We consider him feminine or "queer." In
many men he may evoke fears of sexual involvement which are really
fears of their own unacceptable homosexual tendencies. Such a man
could hardly be the "man's man" of the cigarette advertisements with
a tattoo on the back of his brawny hand—even though the feminine-
appearing man may be a vigorous and effective performer in heterosexual activity.

All of this should point up the extent to which overtly sexual acts
and play are acts of self-expression. This self-expression is an indicator of a person's sense of his own identity. My sexual acts and
involvements say something very important about who I am, how I
perceive myself, what my self-image is. In this, they are sacraments
of my personhood. They are outward and visible signs of the intan-
gible reality which is "me." For example, when I engage in intercourse, I may be saying, among other things, that I perceive myself
as one who requires union with a person of another sex in order to
be fulfilled. If I were to engage in overt homosexual practices, I
might be saying that I perceive myself as one who requires union

with a person of my own sex in order to be fulfilled, or that the most gratifying personal relationships for me are those with members of my own sex. Likewise, if I am engaged in masturbation, I might be saying that I perceive myself as one who, in the interpersonal realm, is in some way self-sufficient. I might also be saying that I fear involvement and self-giving with another person. These illustrations cite overt sexual practices. The point is equally valid for less overt and more common practices, such as flirtation with a member of the opposite sex, or withdrawal from close relationships. In each case, one says something cogent about his real identity.

It is important to recognize that sexual acts are acts of self-expression because of the implications of this recognition for sexual morality. If every sexual act is an expression of me, of who I am, of my identity, then sexual activity itself is deeply personal and interpersonal. It cannot be simply mechanical. Otherwise, it becomes less than full sex. Or, what is being expressed becomes less than full personhood. Mechanical sexual activity (as, for example, in some forms of prostitution) points to a mechanical self-image. It says not only of the partner, but also of myself, that we are not persons, but machines. Sex is objectified as simple release of physiological tension to the point where the subjective dimensions of meaning and relationship are ignored. But the moral considerations which should govern sexual activity are interpersonal rather than mechanical. Right and wrong have more to do with the personal involvement and meaning to which the act points than with mechanical calculations of cause and effect, potential damage to equipment, or even conformity to social rituals. All of these "mechanical" considerations may become morally significant insofar as they have interpersonal implications. But they are not morally significant in and of themselves. Whether or not one is married, for example, he takes seriously the fact that intercourse can lead to pregnancy. This is not because there is anything immoral about pregnancy, but because pregnancy involves the potential life of a person, a person for whom his creators have deep responsibilities. The interpersonal-love basis of morality will be discussed more thoroughly in Chapter 3. It is sufficient here to point out that the final court of appeal in matters of sexual morality derives from the nature of sexual acts themselves. They are personal and interpersonal insofar as they are self-expressive, insofar as they express one's identity.

This is what Paul had in mind when he exhorted the Corinthians to eschew fornication.[23] This is not an indictment of overt sexual acts per se. Neither is it an indictment of any particular incidence of sexual involvement, such as premarital or extramarital intercourse. The Greek word translated "fornication" in that passage (and elsewhere in the New Testament) is *porneia*. It means "misuse of the body." What Paul is saying is consistent with the New Testament love ethic. Bluntly, his exhortation is: "Don't misuse your bodies!" In other words, recognizing that every bodily sexual act is an expression of your self, your personhood, don't "use" your body as if it were a thing. When you do, you are saying that you yourself (to say nothing of your sexual partner) are a thing. You are denying your personhood. And in the process you are depersonalizing sexuality. This eliminates interpersonal love as the final moral consideration, and that is the basis of Paul's indictment. It is significant that the only explicit sexual practice which is indicted in the same passage is prostitution, which generally (although not always) represents the use of the body as a thing. And in the same context Paul says of the body that it is a "temple of the spirit." That is a sacramental understanding of the human body as an outward and visible sign of one's personhood.[24] Bodily acts are therefore personal acts.

ATTITUDES TOWARD THE BODY

This insight into the relationship between bodily acts and self-expression points up the importance of our attitudes toward our bodies. Such attitudes are learned from our environment, through various cultural taboos and mores, as well as prevailing philosophical and theological assumptions. Illustrative of the former are clothing practices which conceal certain parts of the body to the point where they are considered unattractive and viewing them acquires a taboo. Illustrative of the latter is some Greek devaluing of the body in comparison with the soul, and some confused Christian thinking about life after death, which likewise devalues the body.

A particular society is responsible for the attitudes toward the body which it inculcates in its members. Insofar as the church usually functions as a guardian and perpetuator of social mores, this means that the religious establishment bears a large part of this responsibility. The widespread confusion which marks attitudes toward the body on the present American scene is at least partly the fault of the church. This is both tragic and ironic. It is tragic because attitudes toward the body are so central to healthy sexual practices and a viable sexual morality. It is ironic because the church, which rightly assumes responsibility for the encouragement of healthy and moral sexual practices, often promulgates attitudes which inhibit health and morality in the sexual sphere.

There are three basic attitudes toward the human body which are discernible on the contemporary American scene. Actually, these are attitudes toward sexuality itself, because attitudes toward the body usually focus on the parts which most clearly symbolize sexual differentiation. We may classify these three attitudes toward body/ sexuality as "bad," "neutral," and "good." That is, these attitudes assert respectively that the body is bad, the body is neutral, or the body is good. Let us examine each in greater detail. The reader will perhaps identify himself broadly in one of three camps.

The "body/sex is bad" school of thought suffers from embarrassment that human existence involves life in some concrete form. This form is viewed as something of a nonessential, a kind of prison house of the soul, which is the really important dimension of one's being. We have already noted that this attitude is indebted to Greek thought with its dualism of soul and body. Actually, the body here is not only nonessential. It is undesirable. Man is better off when he can shed it, or at least transcend its temptations. Those temptations, which have both mysterious and evil connotations, are focused in the sexual drive and on the parts of the body identified with that drive. According to this view, the body and one's sexuality are at least slightly tainted and dangerous, if not dirty and perverted. This attitude separates body from personhood. It goes under various labels in our time, including the banner of the Christian church. Those who most frequently attack it call it Victorian or Puritanical, often with some unfairness to the doughty pioneers whose images those words evoke. Indeed, these two labels have been so badly abused in the popular sex literature of our time that even the most conservative thinkers pride themselves on being non-Puritanical and post-Victorian!

Regardless of the label, the "sex is bad" school has come in for a good deal of harsh treatment and criticism in recent years. This has come particularly from those who think that the body is a neutral entity, and to some extent from those who are concerned to assert the goodness of the human body. Some critics rightly point out that a negative view of the body can lead to fears of sexual involvement and a negative self-image. It can also lead to self-righteous judgments toward those who are free enough to enjoy their bodies and the pleasures which they yield. Indeed, the criticism of "sex is bad" thinking has risen to such a crescendo in the popular press in recent years that such thinking may become simply a straw man for attacks from both sides in the current debate over sexual morality. This is unfortunate because there is a legitimate basis for the Puritan and Victorian antecedents of "sex is bad" thinking. It lies in the mysterious power of sexuality already cited. To set this line of thinking up as such a straw man that this basis is ignored simply impoverishes thinking on all sides of a profound issue. What needs to be said is that sexuality and the body can not be "bad" as long as both are so central to personal identity. But, by virtue of this centrality, there is a power and mystery to sexuality which makes sexual practices a proper focus of social and moral concern.

Ironically, those who knock the "sex is bad" view the hardest also share in it, and certainly thrive on it. This is particularly true of erotic magazines like *Playboy* which commercialize and trivialize sexuality in the name of a spurious freedom, while loudly proclaiming their crusade against all who think that sex or the body is bad. The irony is that large numbers of those who purchase the *Playboy* product secretly believe that sex really is bad. They purchase the magazine either for moral self-flagellation or for reinforcement of the illusion that they have been emancipated from the bondage which the magazine's editorial policy steadily decries. The vicarious sexual involvement and stimulation which some find in the world of un-reality between the covers of such magazines[25] bears testimony to their continued bondage to "sex is bad" thinking and to the absence of genuine sexual involvement in their lives.

Closely related is the view that the body and sexuality are essentially neutral. They are not bad or dirty, but they remain external to one's personhood. They are only good or bad depending on how they are "used." Adherents of this line of thinking generally consider themselves to have been intellectually emancipated from "sex is bad" thinking. But they persist in the belief that sexuality is basically a thing detached from one's personhood, to be manipulated according to certain pragmatic considerations. On their own pragmatic ground, such thinkers can be just as moralistic and legalistic about sex as the Puritans and Victorians whom they think they have left behind. Indeed, because it has objectified and neutralized sexuality, the "sex/body is neutral" school takes a superficial view which neglects the deep power and mystery of man's sexuality recognized by our forebears. It has already been noted that those who commercialize and trivialize sex often hold this view. Indeed, they frequently consider themselves rather *avant-garde* in it. Actually, the "neutral" attitude toward the body is as old as time and as incomplete as the straw man it sets up in order to justify itself. It can be found in both Plato and St. Paul, although the latter is capable of reaching beyond it in some of his writings.[26] Today, this kind of thinking is the earmark of the would-be intellectual who would like to buttress traditional moral proscriptions with what appears to be up-to-date thinking. Strangely, those who wish to assert a view of the body and sexuality as essentially good find themselves often more violently attacked by "sex is neutral" thinkers than by those whose attitude is determined by their fear of the power of sexuality.

This third view, that sexuality itself is good and to be celebrated, and that one's body is part of the good gift of life, underlies the present essay. It could not be called a popular or prominent attitude, at least in America. There are, however, many who aspire and pretend to it, while harboring a secret suspicion that sex is really bad or at least neutral. And there are a few faithful souls who deeply believe it. Their small number reflects cultural conditioning against acceptance of the goodness and beauty of the human body. Of course, such acceptance involves more demanding moral responsibilities in the realm of sexual self-expression.

Our cultural conditioning is identifiable with an ascetic current in the Christian tradition which can be traced to the Puritan influence on American culture. The point regarding moral responsibility needs elaboration. In what ways is an attitude toward the body which celebrates its wholesomeness more morally demanding than other views? First, it removes the moral escape clause provided by the "sex is bad" line of thinking. This says in effect that since sex is bad and dangerous, all sexual behavior must be governed by rules in the interests of the preservation of society. This relieves the individual of the responsibility to make his own decisions regarding sex. It avoids an agonizing weighing of the demands of love in a given relationship. It also sidesteps the interpersonal implications of sexual acts, both potential and immediate.

Second, insofar as a wholesome attitude toward the body rejects the view that sex is a neutral thing, it avoids basing morality on purely pragmatic considerations. These often simply provide a rationale for the abdication of moral responsibility. To say, for example, that it is all right to engage in intercourse (within or outside marriage) simply because the possibility of pregnancy has been minimized is to evade the invocation of moral ideals and the struggle to act in a way consistent with them. It obscures the interpersonal nature of sexual activity which forms the basis for sexual morality. A view of sexuality and the body as essentially good and central to personhood forces the individual to make sexual decisions on the basis of a person-centered morality. The ultimate value of such a morality is usually called Love, and identified with one or more personal models. Such a morality cannot abdicate responsibility through a flight into legalism. There is always the chance that the dictates of the law may not conform to the demands of Love in a given situation. That is why this morality seems new to those who live under the law. But it is not really new at all. It is as old as its inseparable partner, the view of the body as essentially good which is deeply embedded in the biblical tradition.

Reference has been made to some of the biblical sources of this view, for example, Paul's image of the body as a "temple" of the spirit. A temple is a holy place, a place where the spirit of that which is perceived to be ultimate resides. Therefore, to say that the body is a temple of the human spirit is to say that my body is holy. It is the residence of my personhood. And that personhood itself is the holy of holies in my relationship with others. It is in the image of God.

This biblical view of the body also has implications for a Christian understanding of the Resurrection of the Body. Contrary to pseudo-magical thinking which has infected Christianity from time to time, the Resurrection is not a doctrine of resuscitated corpses. The Resurrection of the Body is rather a way of saying that no spirit has the properties of reality without form. It is a way of saying that to be "me" I must have a body. I cannot be "me" in any other way. You must have a body in order to be a some-body. Otherwise, you are a no-body.

The Resurrection is a mythological image for coming to grips with the spirit/form polarity of human existence. Specifically in relation to Christ, it is a way of saying that the Spirit which he represents cannot be killed. It always survives in a new form. This might be the form of an individual follower of Christ or the form of the institutional church which calls itself the "body of Christ." The relationship of this interpretation of the Resurrection to beliefs about eternal life and life after death is beyond the scope of the present work. The point here is that the body is to be celebrated because it is in the body (in time and space) that one encounters that which is eternal according to biblical faith.

Perhaps the most basic biblical text for the goodness of the body and sexuality is Genesis 1:31, immediately following the creation of man in his bisexual nature: "And God saw everything that he had made, and behold, it was very good." In other words, the whole created order, including and culminating in the sexuality of man, is "very good." That is the basis for the argument of this book that sexuality be viewed within the created order.

2

the exploitation
of sexuality:
sexual immorality

ECAUSE OF THE interpersonal nature of sexual morality the denial of the personal dimension is the fundamental earmark of sexual immorality. This denial may be either explicit or implicit. It is explicit for those who depersonalize sexuality into a crude marketable item. They are not only the technical prostitutes who traffic in their own bodies, but also the journalistic prostitutes who sell the bodies of others across the magazine counter. More often, however, the denial of the personal nature of sexuality is implicit. It is implicit in the mechanical use of bodies which characterizes sex in many marriages, in the "sex for kicks" atmosphere which pervades many college houseparties, and in the view of woman as essentially a toy or playmate according to the Playboy Philosophy. The implicit depersonalization of sexuality is more insidious, for both the individual and society, than the open and explicit exploitation of sex. It is also probably more essentially anti-sex.

When sex is depersonalized it becomes exploitable. This is a circular process, because it is through the continued exploitation of sexuality that it also becomes increasingly dehumanized. To say that sex is exploitable means that it is liable to manipulation in the interests of ends not necessarily related to sexuality itself. Thus, sex can be exploited when it is used exclusively for the release of physiological tension. It can be exploited when it is used for commercial gain. Sex can be exploited when it is used as an emotional weapon against another person. It can be exploited when it is used as a medium for acting out violence against another. The exploitation of sexuality is a focal point for this chapter because it is *the* mark of sexual immorality. This is because it is the handmaid of the dehumanization of sexuality. The two go together. The exploitation of sexuality is the active expression of dehumanized sex.

This chapter is concerned to identify the most prominent expressions of the exploitation of sexuality in our time. Some of these expressions — such as the double standard, the cult of the virgin, and the sexual overtones of racial prejudice — consist primarily of *attitudes* which promote the exploitation of sexuality. More often than not, such attitudes are themselves perpetuated by identifiable interest-groups within a society. However, frequently those who promote these attitudes are as much victimized as victimizing. Other expressions of the exploitation of sexuality, such as its marketing and the use of sex as a weapon of violence, represent practices closely related to exploitative attitudes. All such practices fall under the broad heading of the misuse of the body, the focus of Paul's indictment in the passage in the sixth chapter of First Corinthians.

It is worth noting what is *not* the focus of this chapter on sexual immorality. What is not focused reveals as much about our moral point of departure as what is focused. This chapter does not zero in on premarital intercourse, homosexuality, masturbation, adultery and other carefully defined forms of sexual expression. These forms of behavior may or may not be immoral depending on a variety of factors, including the context in which they are indulged, the meaning of the act to the participants, and the foreseeable consequences. All of these factors may finally be reduced to the question of whether or not sexuality itself is depersonalized and exploited. When that happens, Love, which is the assumed norm for all morality, is ruled out of court as a moral criterion.

SEX AND THE MARKETPLACE

One of the most obvious exploitations of sexuality appears in the relationship between sex and the marketplace. Sex virtually dominates the marketplace in our time, and vice versa. Sexuality is probably the most easily marketable item in our culture, as well as the most successful accessory for marketing anything else. At the same time, a marketing orientation increasingly permeates our perception of our sexuality. On the former count, unconcealed sexual imagery and the most unsubtle promises of sexual fulfillment are used to sell everything from deodorant to cigars, to say nothing of the extent to which sex itself sells in the world of journalism. On the latter count, we teach our children from an early age to place a market value on their sexuality and to value sexual attractiveness accordingly. They learn that superficial sexual attractiveness, whether or not the promise which it holds out is realizable, provides entrée to relationships with people who count, better prospects in finding a mate, greater job potential, and even (according to some advertising) a better chance of getting into college! In short, sexual attractiveness has become one of the primary access routes to the fulfillment of the American dream of "getting ahead."

Indeed, the crass marketing of sexuality has become such a popular whipping boy that one is tempted to avoid it as a focus of sexual immorality. Still, in a society as thoroughly sex-saturated and as uncritically profit-oriented as our own, the combination of these two tendencies is as inevitable for our culture as it is inescapable for any critical analyst. What is depressing is the vicious circle which the prevailing relationship between sex and marketing represents. As long as large segments of our society remain sex-starved (i.e., deprived of genuine interpersonal sexual encounter), the mass media of the society will continue to be sex-saturated. And as long as that situation prevails in a society which survives economically by inducing its members to purchase things they don't need, the marriage between sex and the marketplace will remain indissoluble. This prostitution of sexuality in the cognitive signals we daily receive contributes in its turn to the prolonging of the sex famine of the American public.

The commercial exploitation of sex involves both the objectification and the dehumanization of human sexuality. It involves the objectification of sexuality because nothing can be sold (or used to sell) as long as it retains in the mind of buyer or seller its nature as subject. This "natural" morality can be illustrated in a number of ways. The institution of slavery, for example, represents an objectifying of persons for commercial purposes. But the tenaciously long life of slavery would not have been possible if men had not anesthetized themselves morally by objectifying slaves. This was accomplished by assuming that they were something less than human, by refusing to recognize their essential subjectivity. This kind of moral anesthesia underlies the vestiges of deep-seated racial feelings among whites in those areas where people have been taught for too long that Negroes really are something less than human. It is significant that the moral protest which finally undercut the slave trade came from the community of faith in which some take seriously the teaching that every man is a unique subject (soul/self).

Likewise, any pet lover knows the feeling of moral ambiguity which usually attends the buying and selling of domestic animals. This is because pets become for their owners subjects. They become personalized. Interpersonal-like relations are established with them and human-like traits, including the essential subjectivity of human nature, are projected onto them. When this happens, the prospect of the commercial use of a pet, such as the gainful sale of offspring or some professional showing of animals, evokes feelings of moral ambiguity. These feelings are ambiguous because pets are clearly not human subjects, yet are often related to as human subjects. People who show dogs professionally and animal trainers in commercial shows, for example, testify that it is necessary for them to maintain some distance and aloofness in their relationships with the animals they train. What they are saying is that it is necessary for them to objectify the animal, so to speak to mechanize him, to guard

against assigning him any meaningful subjectivity. This would interfere with his commercial use.

Likewise with human sexuality. Unless it is objectified to the
point where its essential subjectivity, its person-centeredness, is suppressed or ignored, natural human sensibilities will not tolerate its
commercial exploitation. That such moral sensitivity may be a function of fears of becoming an object oneself does not reduce its moral
power. Indeed, the difficulty we have objectifying those with whom
we identify attests to the basic interpersonal nature of morality. And
the apparent ease with which modern man exploits his sexuality
commercially likewise points to his failure to "feel" the personal
dimension of his sexuality. He has objectified it. It is a detached
thing rather than a fundamental dimension of his being human.

Herein lies the connection between the objectification and the
dehumanization of sexuality. Depersonalization is simply a subtle
and less crass form of objectification. It represents a process of
thinking we apply with particular effectiveness to our enemies, sup-
posed and real. However, it is equally necessary to the commercial
exploitation of anyone. Depersonalization allows that the other
person is a human being, but only in a peripheral way. He is somehow not as human as I am. And certainly his human interests and
rights are not as important as mine. For example, the emergence of
the war in Vietnam evoked among the American people a tendency
to dehumanize the people of Vietnam. This happened not because
most of us had anything explicitly against those people. It developed because our own national and personal self-interest demanded
(for at least some) that we wreak havoc and suffering on the people
of Vietnam. That this particular people is racially distinguishable
from us made it easier to apply the moral anesthesia of dehumanization. It was likewise easier in 1945 to drop the atomic bomb on
Orientals in Hiroshima and Nagasaki than on Caucasians in Berlin.
We do, however, even dehumanize people of the same race when
our moral sensibilities demand it. We dehumanized the German
enemy during World War II through the caricature of the monocle

and Prussian rigidity, just as more recently the boorish caricature of the Russian has made it easier for large numbers of Americans to fear and hate him.

The dehumanization of sexuality is simply the refusal to let personal considerations interfere with the ways in which we use our sexuality, just as the dehumanization of the Vietnamese was the refusal to let personal considerations interfere with the ways in which he was used as a political pawn. Where the commercialization of sex is involved, dehumanization is the price we must pay in order that personal considerations not interfere.

The question, however, remains: Why is sex so easily marketable in the first place? How are we to explain the tremendous appeal of sex on the American market? Its virtual centrality to the American economy? Its power to inspire otherwise irrational buying patterns? The answer to those questions should be as obvious as the fact that the price of food soars in times of famine. There is an incessant demand for authentic sexual fulfillment in our time. Although that demand is stimulated by the sex motif in the mass media, its roots lie not in abundance of riches but in real sexual poverty. Sex sells big because people are starved for it. And the more phoney, objectified sex they get on the market, the more frantic their starvation becomes, and the more they buy.

Ironically, the church which decries the commercialization of sex, has done its own share to make it a marketable item. In misguided moral zeal, the church has promulgated attitudes toward sexuality and the body which tend to objectify the former and separate the latter from its essential subjectivity, its soul. One of these attitudes bases sexual morality on a fear of the dangers of sex rather than a celebration of its glories. The church has too often allowed concerns for the preservation of society to seduce it into emphasizing fear of sexuality to the neglect of its potential. This results in a negative view of sex and the body and in a negative morality. Such a morality is based more on the fear of sin than on the potential of its opposite number, Love. This makes sex a marketable item because it suppresses genuine sexual involvement and fulfillment, and also because it demonizes and objectifies sex. The church then has made its own unique contribution to the sexual starvation of our time. It continues to promote the famine whenever it preaches a morality based on fear (or its sophisticated counterpart, prudence) rather than the power of Love.

Illustrative is the response of many churchmen to pornography. *Pornography* means literally "pictures [graphs] of the misuse of the body [*porneia*]." In the pornographic literature which abounds on the American scene, such pictures may be verbal as well as graphic. The legal complexities of defining pornography notwithstanding, most would agree that contemporary American society produces its ample share of pornographic literature. The question on which it is difficult to find agreement is whether the widespread availability of pornography is a symptom or a cause of the sexual sickness of our society. And within the church, with its sexual morality based on fear, there has been a tendency to respond to pornography as if it were the problem, rather than simply a symptom — and a relatively innocuous one at that. One church has, for example, devoted a large amount of time and energy to a war on pornography, including the mobilization of members to check on stores selling such literature and to prod their legislators on this issue. This sincere but misguided zeal has borne little fruit, primarily because it is an attempt to cure an illness by eliminating its symptoms. Not only does pornography effectively survive such attacks (with or without the legal protection it generally enjoys), but the sickness of which pornography is a symptom thrives on the medication. In our already sex-starved society, any moralist's attempt to stamp out pornography has about the same effect on popular demand as the banning of a book in Boston has on its marketability. By attacking pornography as if it were the sickness instead of one symptom, well-intentioned churchmen have often escalated its market and aggravated, rather than alleviated, such problems as it may pose for society. Ironically, the fears on which their moral zeal is usually based, that pornography can lead to the moral corruption of otherwise innocent children, seem to be largely unfounded. It is unlikely that a dirty picture will corrupt anyone's morals any more than the smell of whiskey will create an alcoholic, as some teetotalers still think.

Pornography itself, like the other forms under which sex is hawked in the modern marketplace, is clearly an exploitation of sexuality and an expression of the sexual immorality of our time. But it is no more exploitative than the subtle sexual innuendos and promises which mark most advertising. Indeed, insofar as hard pornography is crass and undevious, it may be less exploitative of sexuality in the long run than the bulk of popular advertising. Those who would launch witch-hunts for the hawkers of pornography might do well to count how many pillars of their own church or community are involved in such subtle forms of the exploitation of sexuality as advertising, promotion, and journalism.

What provides a market for pornography is a sex-starved society which has been nurtured on the objectification and dehumanization of sexuality. In such a society, increasingly large numbers of people will find that they can "get their kicks" out of the kind of depersonalized sex which is the only sex that pornographic journals can deliver. And more alarming is that increasing numbers of people may find that this kind of vicarious sexual involvement is the only way they *can* get their kicks. They may find that they have come to have such a negative and objective image of their own sexuality that an authentic, personal sexual encounter is unlikely.

Pornography is then in a real sense the ultimate expression of the relationship between sex and the marketplace. Like prostitution, it is a rather crass and basic form of the commercial exploitation of sexuality. But like prostitution also, pornography does not make a society morally sick. It is a parasite which presupposes and requires a society already morally sick and sexually confused. Without such a climate, the parasite withers and atrophies, as has been demonstrated in countries like Sweden where healthier and more positive attitudes toward sexuality prevail than in America.

THE DOUBLE STANDARD

One attitude which affects the climate in which pornography can flourish is the sexual double standard. The double standard teaches basically that the canons of sexual morality are different for men than for women. It is an outmoded vestige of a patriarchal world-view, but one which is still very much a part of a mid-twentieth-century frame of reference.

The double standard has various political, economic, and even physiological nuances which are beyond the scope of the present work. Its basic immorality and depersonalizing tendencies, however, are demonstrated by two of its fundamental earmarks. One of these is its moral hypocrisy. The other is its implicit view of sexual differentiation and the evaluative distinction which it draws between male and female humanness.

The moral hypocrisy of the sexual double standard requires little elaboration. It is usually acknowledged even by those, such as school administrators and clergy, who support policies which tend to perpetuate the double standard. The double standard is hypocritical because it openly teaches that there are different moral standards in the realm of sex for different classes of human beings. At the same time, it pretends to allow that women are as human as men. But the double standard implicitly assumes that women are not really quite as human as men. Consequently, they are not entitled to the full human rights which men enjoy, especially in the sexual realm.

It is assumed, for example, that women cannot be as free in their sexual expression as men. This applies not only to the premarital sexual license which is tacitly extended to men by the double standard but also to freedom in the variety of sexual partners before and (to some extent) after marriage. It often applies to freedom of expression in the sexual act itself. It even applies to deep-seated attitudes toward overt female homosexuality and masturbation.[1]

It is also often assumed under the double standard that the sexual needs of women are not as great as those of men, an expression of masculine sexual naïveté which there is now considerable clinical evidence to contradict.[2] Accordingly, women are assigned a greater share of moral responsibility for regulating the extent and type of heterosexual play before marriage.[3] And the female body is degraded by socially unacceptable sex with a stigma and permanence that is not extended to the male body for similar involvements.[4]

Following the same reasoning, women are viewed as requiring society's protection from the sexually more avaricious male. This assumption is used to justify sexual restrictions and taboos on women, just as restrictions on the voting rights of the American Negro are still sometimes justified on the grounds that he is being protected from exploitation! These restrictions usually assume that women are somehow incapable of exercising the responsible choice necessary for sexual self-protection. This view is ironic since it generally goes hand in hand with the assignment of greater premarital sexual responsibility to women.

All of these assumptions express and reinforce the moral hypocrisy of the double standard. They also point to a dehumanizing of women which denies the basicness of sexual differentiation to human nature. The view of maleness and femaleness which pervades double standard thinking is one of masculine superiority. There are two distinct orders of human being, and the male order is clearly superior — morally, physically, and intellectually. Such thinking plays havoc with the holistic view of sexual differentiation urged in Chapter 1. It points toward the assumption that the male is self-sufficiently human. And the female is one of many objects in his environment which he may use to gratify his needs, within socially prescribed limits. The offensiveness of sexual segregation, when presented in such terms, should not blind us to the extent to which it is still a reality. As long as the double standard continues to inform our thinking, we cannot plead that the indictment of the above description is an exaggeration.

Anyone who has spent much time on college campuses or with young adults knows the insidious effect which the double standard has on their sexual attitudes and practices. A male undergraduate comments, for example, in regard to his fraternity brothers: "They can do anything they want as long as they don't do it to my sister or the girl I'm going to marry." And the double standard also has a deep effect on sexual attitudes and practices among young unmarried women. This is true whether a girl submits to or rebels against the double standard. No small number of young women are frozen into one form or another of sexual inadequacy by the dire threats which the double standard carries. But no small number also precipitate meaningless sexual liaisons in an attempt to prove that they have been emancipated from the double standard. Such compulsive rebellion is usually abortive and demonstrates bondage rather than the freedom it is intended to signify. And it practices the same kind of exploitation which the double standard encourages.

In spite of growing recognition of the debilitating effects of the double standard, it continues to be reinforced legally and socially. Two areas of reinforcement are the availability of birth control devices and the proprietary rules for women at most undergraduate colleges.

Popular attitudes and practices regarding birth control represent perhaps the clearest area in which double standard thinking is reinforced. It occurs to very few, for example, to note the discrepancy between the ease with which a man may procure a prophylactic (in some states through washroom dispensers) and a woman may procure birth control pills or a vaginal diaphragm (by medical prescription only). Our insensitivity to such injustice attests to the degree to which we are steeped in double standard thinking. Whatever the medical reasons for this discrepancy, the law in effect discriminates against unmarried women. This leads to a dilemma for those who counsel professionally with women. Female devices are demonstrably more effective, and unmarried women are often determined to have them, even if it means circumventing normal procedures. This can be simply for self-protection against the stigma of an unmarried pregnancy, another expression of double standard thinking. But also, increasing numbers of young unmarried women appear to be procuring such devices whether or not they have immediate prospects for their use. This pattern bears particularly unjustly on the medical practitioner who finds himself in a moral double bind. His only alternatives appear to be withholding a more reliable method of conception-prevention (where the foreseeable consequences of conception could be personally and socially disastrous) or being an accomplice to tabooed behavior. It is a credit to the moral integrity of many doctors that they recognize the hypocrisy of the double standard and opt for the latter alternative. But that does not make them any the less victims of the double standard. It puts them in a position where they are "damned if they do and damned if they don't." The choice usually comes down to whether they prefer being damned by their own conscience or damned by a morally hypocritical society, although unfortunately the choice is not always that clear.

The same may be said of the proprietary regulations for women still enforced by the vast majority of undergraduate colleges. These are nothing less than discriminatory. They reflect the double standard at its worst. Not only are they unjust, but they also can serve to inhibit college women from learning to exercise real moral responsibility for their lives. And yet it still occurs to relatively few to question the discrepancy between the "hours" imposed on undergraduate women, generally through their senior year, and the social freedom which undergraduate men enjoy in most institutions as freshmen. There is something incongruous in there being greater social restrictions for a mature, sexually eligible young woman of twenty-one than for a fuzzy-faced, barely post-puberty young man of seventeen. And yet earnest and reasonably well-informed college administrators continue to intone platitudes about being their brother's keeper and about *in loco parentis* responsibilities. The irony is that colleges do have a responsibility in the moral/social realm to their undergraduates, but it is fundamentally the same for men as for women. And colleges do assume an *in loco parentis* role. But that role, like the role of a good parent, should be interpreted, not as the enforcement of social restrictions, but as providing a climate for growth— to moral as well as intellectual maturity.

The responsibility which most colleges' proprietary rules for women really express is to the society on which the college is dependent for financial support. Again, it is true that our institutions of higher learning have a responsibility to the society which supports them and which they exist to serve. But that responsibility might be interpreted more critically than it often is. It need not be a responsibility simply to submit college policies to public opinion. It might instead be interpreted as a prophetic responsibility to reform public opinion with policies which challenge prevailing mores. Nowhere do our colleges have a greater opportunity to fulfill such a role today than in the realm of the sexual double standard which they so often serve to perpetuate. If more of our colleges would give to the human relations among their students the attention they now give to their own public relations, academia might reemerge in the prophetic role it is uniquely fitted to serve. Then it would be exercising real moral responsibility, that of a public conscience, toward the society in which it finds itself.

In this, the analogy between the educational establishment and the religious establishment, between *academia* and *ecclesia,* is striking. The *raison d'être* of each is highly idealistic — for the one, the pursuit of Truth, for the other the proclamation and practice of Love. Yet each has contributed in its own way to the sexual dishonesty of our time. And each includes in its charter that potential independence of the social order whereby it might be more constructively critical, rather than simply mirroring the moral confusion of the status quo.

We should not be surprised then at the tenacity of the double standard, even in a time when its anachronistic dimensions are becoming increasingly evident. It is, like the depersonalization of which it is an instrument, a function of the exploitation of sexuality. As such, it will probably be with us as long as human sexuality remains such a central focus of man's inhumanity to man. It will be with us at least until sexual man accepts the full humanity (and sexuality) of sexual woman.

THE CULT OF THE VIRGIN

Sexuality is also exploited by the modern cult of the virgin. This is a mind-set which reveres virginity, particularly in the unmarried female. When this reverence borders on worship, with all of its mystical connotations, we may identify it as a cult. It has clear religious overtones, as revealed, for example, in the mystical significance ascribed to the loss of one's technical virginity. Insofar as this mystique reflects the interpersonal nature of the heterosexual act, it is appropriate. Insofar as it focuses on the loss of virginity per se, it is idolatrous. This idolatry has caused untold numbers of young women, and no small number of young men, to suffer pangs of remorse, self-doubt, and guilt because the stars did not change their orbit on the occasion of their first intercourse. In this, the cult of the virgin practices the same kind of deception as the cult of the sacrament within the church, where the letdown feeling of confirmands after their first communion is analogous to the letdown of many brides on their wedding night.

The cult of the virgin also has religious roots. At the most obvious level, it is encouraged by the teaching of the church with its explicit reservation of intercourse for marriage and the symbolism of most religious wedding ceremonies — the pure white costume of the bride and her father's giving her away to her husband. At another level, the cult of the virgin is particularly an expression of the Christian tradition in which sexual chastity has been interpreted as a sign of godliness. One of the ironies of contemporary church life, particularly within American Protestantism, is that where the injunction to chastity in the threefold monastic vow has been so emphasized, the injunctions to poverty and radical obedience have been almost wholly ignored. Any genuine monastic knows that such a separation is idolatrous, that the vows are interdependent, and that you can't have one without the others.

At a deeper psychic and emotional level, the cult of the virgin has also been fostered in the Christian tradition by a focus on what is assumed to have been the sexless life of a "spotless" Savior.[5] This is exacerbated by the cult of the Virgin Mary, which teaches that the birth of such a sinless one must be "without spot" of sexual involvement. The high place assigned to Mary within Roman Catholicism may aggravate this problem. But Protestants, even with their refusal to worship at her shrine, pay her lip service in their prevailing attitudes toward virginity. The real theological significance of Mary in Scripture is not her virginity, but her obedience: "Be it unto me according to your word."[6] And the real theological significance of the myth of the virgin birth has nothing to do with sex and very little to do with Mary. It has to do with Jesus, and represents an attempt to set him forth as the fulfillment of Old Testament prophecy,[7] and to dramatize what the early church believed to be his nature as the God-man.

The fundamental heresy of the cult of the virgin is its identification of technical virginity with chastity. This equates refusal or inability to engage in sexual relations with cleanliness, purity, godliness. It not only casts aspersions on those who engage in such acts. It also asserts the moral superiority of the celibate. The proper understanding, however, has always been, not that it is morally superior to be a eunuch, but that it is morally superior to be a eunuch "for the kingdom's sake."[8] And the difference is as important as that between simply dying on the one hand and giving up one's life for a moral ideal on the other.

This identification of virginity with chastity and moral superiority has implications for morality, for patterns of sexual behavior, particularly among young unmarried people, and for the view of the body which we teach our children. What are some of these implications? How do they manifest themselves?

In the realm of morality, we have seen that sexual abstention is assigned a certain cleanliness and moral value. In such thinking, the rationale for sexual abstention is rarely taken into consideration. The moral value is ascribed to the abstention itself, to the form rather than the spirit of one's behavior. That is consistent with the idolatry of virginity which characterizes the cult of the virgin. In the same way, the legalist's hyper-concern with the letter rather than the spirit of the law is consistent with his idolatrous attitude toward the letter of any moral code. The corollary of ascribing moral superiority to abstention is the assumption that overt sexual involvement of any kind is at least slightly tainted. It is tolerated by society, but primarily because it is recognized as necessary to the preservation of the species, and is experienced as virtually impossible to stamp out. It is tolerated because it is the lesser of two evils. This is the weight of

Paul's somewhat confused dictum that it is better to marry than to burn.[9] That statement assumes the imminent end of the world, and reflects the logical outcome of virgin-cult thinking when the preservation of the species is removed as a justification for sexual involvement. The implications of the cult of the virgin for sexual morality are then both clear and insidious. It teaches that sex itself is a necessary evil and that its subjugation and denial is a virtue. And it provides us with a shallow and unrealistic yardstick for moral integrity.

The lack of moral integrity which the cult of the virgin encourages is reflected in the behavior patterns of those who take it seriously. The most dubious of these patterns is the maintenance of "technical virginity." A technical virgin is one who has refrained from what is defined in graphic terms as sexual intercourse. Such a person considers himself or herself a virgin and enjoys all the questionable privileges and status of that state. He may, however, regularly engage in other forms of heterosexual play which are in some ways more personal and intimate than intercourse. Common among these forms are petting to orgasm and oral-genital contacts. There is, of course, nothing essentially moral or immoral about either of these practices or a number of other gymnastics indulged in by those who feel called to protect their technical virginity. But the assumption that such practices are moral because they do not destroy technical virginity is symptomatic of moral confusion. It also undercuts a person-centered basis for sexual morality, effectively downgrades interpersonal love as a moral consideration, and reflects the genital preoccupation of our time.

The moral judgment which the cult of the virgin passes on such behavior is not the only problem in this area. What is most damaging to a person-centered morality is that the cult encourages such forms of sexual expression in the name of morality. Thus, to many young people, intimacies which are often inappropriate to their relationship and for which they are emotionally ill-prepared seem to be the only morally acceptable culmination of sexual play. The encouragement of, for example, oral-genital contact in those who are neither emotionally prepared nor affectionately inclined to such levels of involvement can lead to emotional scars, revulsion at one's own sexuality, and lasting alienation from the opposite sex. If man is dependent for fulfillment on a real relationship with his opposite sexual number, any attitude which encourages such alienation must be viewed as an expression of sexual immorality and depersonalization.

Finally, the implicit view of the body in the cult of the virgin should be clear. To make virginity itself a moral criterion is to focus one's sexual identity in his genitals, since that is where virginity is exclusively counted. It also implies that the genitalia are themselves tainted or morally corrupt, insofar as their non-use is morally superior to their use. Where body/flesh means genitals, and where genitals are the focus of moral fears and taboos, the outcome is a view of the body as a moral encumbrance. The body then becomes the seat of temptations which seduce man away from the moral perfection of which his (apparently disembodied) soul is assumed to be capable. The same view is reflected in the exploitation of sexuality by popular advertising and the marketing orientation of prevailing sexual attitudes. Harvey Cox has provided a perceptive and entertaining analysis of the extent to which this attitude informs the annual Miss America pageant. He rightly sees the pageant as a ritual in the worship of virginity and a depersonalized body.[10] And he points out that for many Americans Miss America is a surrogate goddess, a living symbol of the spotless and untouchable virginity they worship. One might also add that she has become *the* symbol of the marketability of sex in our time. Witness the income she can glean from endorsing the most trivial products with her virgin-white smile or her immaculate body. And she also stands as living proof of the relationship between sexual attractiveness and success in our society.

Insofar as the cult of the virgin is primarily feminine, it is, of course, closely related to the double standard. As such, it is another attitudinal foundation-stone of the exploitation of sexuality and a symptom of the sexual immorality of our time.

SEX AND RACE

Related to the cult of the virgin is the extent to which depersonalizing sexual attitudes inform our current racial ferment. The relationship between sexual and racial attitudes is as frequently ignored
in discussions of the racial issue as in discussions of our sexual
malaise. This is surprising because no one who has done civil rights
work is unaware of this relationship. And those who most vehe-
mently oppose the guaranteeing of civil rights to Negroes explicitly
proclaim it.

Ask an overt segregationist about his deepest racial feelings and
fears, and he will usually respond in terms of the prospects of a
black man sleeping with a white woman. The "natural" horror of
many white men (and not in the South alone) at this eventuality is
akin to the horror of incest, which Freud rightly saw as not natural
but socially conditioned.[11] Likewise, the egalitarian spirit among
those actively working for civil rights is proclaimed, among other
things, in terms of acceptance of interracial sex. That this acceptance is occasionally acted out attests to the extent to which sex is
a basic proving ground for one's ideological affirmations in the racial
realm. Failure to acknowledge just how basic sexual attitudes are
to the present racial issue has served to make sex the great hidden
agenda in the civil rights controversy. As a colleague once put it:
"The two great issues for students today are sex and civil rights,
usually in that order and usually related!"

Morally speaking, the relationship between sexual attitudes and
racial attitudes is a two-edged sword. On the one hand, in recognizing it and coping with it constructively lies one of the pathways
to genuine acceptance by whites of the full humanity of Negroes,
and vice versa. The acknowledgement of the sexual attractiveness
of another human being, regardless of race, can be one step toward
an acknowledgement of the personal attractiveness of that being.
And growing acceptance of interracial sexual involvement and marriage will be a blow to the depersonalization of the Negro which
current taboos and fears reflect. The white man who fears that progressive integration of educational facilities will lead to increased

interracial sexual involvement is right in his prognosis, wrong in fearing it. With more social contact at increasingly early ages (before depersonalizing stereotypes can be established on either side), there will be an increase in sexual involvement between the races. This can only be a cause for alarm among those whites who are persuaded that the Negro represents an inferior brand of humanity and there-fore poses a kind of mongrelizing threat to the Caucasian strain. This is precisely what many white supremacists believe. That Negro civil rights leaders have generally soft-pedaled this eventuality be-speaks their estimate of its emotional power to inhibit their move-ment. Likewise, white supremacist exaggerations of this prospect show recognition of its emotional power to swing public opinion in the direction of their own biases.

The relationship between sex and race can lead then to exploita-tion of both sexuality and "raciality." Both the sexuality and the personhood of the Negro were exploited by the white plantation owner who, according to popular legend, "used" his women slaves for his own sexual gratification. But sexuality and personhood are also exploited by those who engage in interracial sex in order to demonstrate their emancipation from traditional taboos. Like most attempts to demonstrate emancipation and freethinking, this usu-ally demonstrates the opposite. It shows such bondage to the old taboos that one must act out his violation of them in order to per-suade himself and others that he has broken the bondage. This can also betoken, of course, bondage to the popular egalitarian image rather than loyalty to true egalitarian, person-centered values.

The depersonalization of the Negro in white fears of his sexuality, however, runs even deeper. For example, these fears are most often articulated in terms of the prospects of sexual involvement between a black man and a white woman, not vice versa. This reflects two attitudes. First, it reveals the assumption that women in general are property. A colored woman therefore is an appropriate object for a white man's sexual gratification not simply because she is a Negro, but because she is a woman. Likewise, a white woman is the general property of white men, even if she has no specific white lover, and

regardless of her own feelings toward Negro men. She is not therefore to be *defiled* by a Negro man, who is, of course, inferior to a
white man. The whole charade of southern justice, as reflected, for
example, in Harper Lee's *To Kill a Mockingbird*,[12] shows this bias.
This bias is also reflected in revulsion toward a white woman who
willingly sleeps with a Negro.

A second assumption is that the Negro is more akin sexually to
an animal than to a human being. This is reflected in popular southern white lore concerning the sexual prowess of the Negro, both male
and female. Insofar as the white man derives vicarious enjoyment
from myths of the Negro's sexual prowess, this may be a projection
of the powers to which he aspires and of his own fears of sexual
inadequacy. Where the Negro is viewed as a subhuman animal with
superhuman sexual power it should not be surprising that the prospect of his involvement with a white woman evokes feelings of revulsion and hostility. At the same time, intercourse between a white
man and a Negro woman can be almost cavalierly admired as the
conquest of a particularly enticing and gratifying sexual object. In
the poor white subculture of the Northeast, young men are raised
with the myth that "you're not a man until you've split black oak."
A telling analogy is the mild fascination evoked by stories of sexual
experimentation by farm boys on the livestock, compared with the
horror which would greet accounts of sexual involvement between
one of the livestock and a farm girl!

It seems clear that the relationship between race and sex informs
prevailing attitudes in both realms. These attitudes can be instru-
ments of a subtle but nonetheless real exploitation of sexuality and
persons. As such, they are another expression of the fundamental
sexual immorality of our time.

SEX AND VIOLENCE

Also frequently ignored in discussions of sexual morality is the
relationship between sex and violence. This relationship can be
intricate. At the most obvious level, the sexual act is, for example,
often accompanied by some form of violence. Clinicians tell us that

it is not uncommon for individuals to derive considerable erotic satisfaction from being the objects as well as the perpetrators of such violence.[13] This had led to a recognition of the sadomasochistic dimension of sexual activity, which may be fundamental to the phenomena of sadism and masochism in all human relationships.

Not as commonly acknowledged, however, is the extent to which violence serves as a surrogate for authentic sexual involvement. Likewise, sexual activity can serve as a surrogate for the expression of violent needs. That the relationship between sex and violence is rarely recognized should not be surprising in light of our general unwillingness to acknowledge how violence-saturated contemporary American culture is. Those who are not persuaded by apparently meaningless mass killings can consult their daily papers or turn on their television sets to see what a prominent place accounts of violence are accorded in the mass media. This reflects a widespread, although generally unconscious, public demand for accounts of violence. Given the marketing orientation of the mass media, if the bloody western gunfight will sell more breakfast cereal than the speeches of Hamlet, then gunfights are what the American people are going to be fed. Likewise, if vivid accounts of a hatchet slaying will sell more newspapers than the proceedings of a disarmament conference, one does not need to guess which story will get a bigger play on the front page.

This thirst for violence betokens a need for vicarious expressions of violence, since its overt expression is still generally unacceptable (except where it is ritually justified, as, for example, in war and in certain athletic events). A violence-saturated society is therefore also a violence-starved society. This is one of the parallels between current attitudes toward violence and sex. Just as a society starved for authentic sexual involvement grasps at inauthentic, vicarious sex in its advertising, journalism, and literature, so a society starved for socially acceptable channels for violence grasps for vicarious violence in the same media. Actually, the two phenomena are not only parallel but related, insofar as sexual frustration is one root of tendencies toward violence.

Another parallel between attitudes toward violence and sexuality is reflected in the high marketability of violence. The promise or portrayal of violence ranks second only to sex in its capacity to open the American pocketbook. In this, apparently innocuous children's comic books which portray acts of interpersonal violence may represent the true pornography of our time. They might be a more appropriate target for those moral zealots who would eliminate the literary or journalistic portrayal of immoral acts. Also, vicarious violence, like vicarious sex, is depersonalizing. The cowboy who lies in a pool of his own blood or the hoodlum who emits a blood-curdling scream as he is dropped from the roof by a sharpshooting G-man is no more a real human being than the popular "playmate of the month" or the misty-eyed wench who exudes sex all over her boyfriend's properly chosen cigar. And it is only one short step from vicarious participation in such portrayals to the experience of the American flyer who attests that "bombing is a clean way to fight a war because you're destroying things down there, not people" and the would-be sophisticate who makes little if any distinction between the ways in which he treats his girlfriend and his sports car.

Violence in sex, violence as a surrogate for sex, and sex as a surrogate for violence—all are dimensions of the exploitation of sexuality. Of course, there is a natural violence of bodily expression which attends extreme sexual excitement, best illustrated in the spasmodic nature of most sexual orgasm. But this is different from finding fulfillment in the inflicting or receiving of violence in the sexual act. The latter is a misuse of sexuality which is as tragic and constricting as it is distorted. Likewise, where violence becomes a surrogate for sexual actvity, not only the personhood of another but one's own personhood is exploited. Authentic sexual fulfillment is upstaged by a poor substitute. The corollary use of sex to fulfill needs for violence subjugates the interpersonal dimension of sexual involvement to a particular function, and is exploitative of sexuality itself.

A more open acknowledgement of the relationship between sex and violence could be an attack on the sexual immorality of our time. It will probably not come about, however, until we are willing to question the morality of the violence which our society regularly condones—from making war to various police tactics to capital punishment to certain popular spectator sports.

CONCLUSION: THE MISUSE OF THE BODY

The cult of the virgin and the relationships between sex and race and between sex and violence all point up the extent to which sexuality is focused in the body. Our discussion of sexual immorality has now come full cycle. The discussion begins and ends with the assertion that the fundamental earmark of sexual immorality is the misuse of the body. Although there are nonsexual forms of the misuse of the body (for example, over-consumption of food, alcohol, tobacco, and drugs), which must also be viewed as immoral,[14] in the sexual realm the misuse of the body is virtually indistinguishable from the exploitation of one's sexuality.

Someone may ask at this point: "But what is the criterion by which one determines what is and what is not misuse of the body?" That is a legitimate question. Without the following chapter, which attempts to spell out a viable standard for sexual ethics, the foregoing discussion might be dismissed as moralistic and negativistic, as making no constructive contribution to the search for a meaningful sexual morality. It remains to the chapter which follows to elaborate the criterion (Love) by which the individual determines what is and is not the misuse of his body and the bodies of others. This is because the ethical attitude assumed throughout this work is thoroughly contextual. That means that what is misuse of the body and the exploitation of sexuality for one man is not for another. Prostitution, for example, for a New York call girl and for the joyful and self-giving heroine of the movie *Never On Sunday* may mean quite different things. What is misuse of the body in the context of one relationship may not be in another. For instance, oral-genital love-making may be appropriate to a relationship in which it is a natural and voluntary form of self-expression. It could be immoral where it is a surrogate for that which is tabooed, or a source of guilt and revulsion to those who practice it. A particular form of sexual activity which is exploitative in one cultural context may not be in another. Polygamy in Samoa may have a different meaning and function from polygamy in Scarsdale. Such a contextual ethical attitude is coterminous with the so-called new morality, which is our moral point of departure.

Let the reader be reminded that the exploitation of sexuality as a basic definition of sexual immorality reflects the Pauline teaching which has been cited earlier. It remains now to elaborate the positive moral norm which underlies Paul's teaching and is reflected in his view of the body as a temple. That norm is the love revealed in the personhood (including the bodily form) of Jesus of Nazareth. What makes the body a temple for this Love/God is that the body serves as *the* mediator of interpersonal love. Therefore, where the misuse of the body is identified as the earmark of sexual immorality, the "proper" use of the body must be viewed as the earmark of sexual morality. If sexual immorality is defined in terms of the exploitation of sexuality, sexual morality must be defined in terms of the realization of sexuality.

If sex is as basic to human identity as posited in Chapter 1, the realization of one's sexuality amounts to the realization of one's personhood. That is a laudable moral goal. It represents an appropriate translation of the alleged words of Jesus: "I have come that they may have life, and have it abundantly."[15]

3

the realization
of sexuality:
sexual morality

OUR ARGUMENT has sought to identify the symptoms of sexual immorality in our time before setting forth a moral framework. Of course, experientially, in the myriad decisions we all make, the order is usually the reverse. We hold to some more-or-less-conscious moral framework and hierarchy of values, and on the basis of that "morality" determine what is moral or immoral in a given situation. But too many discussions of morality suffer from high-blown theorizing which is never illustrated concretely. Or the illustrations are provided only after the fact so that the reader either subscribes to or rejects the theoretical framework on purely logical rather than experiential grounds. This is a problem for the current debate between "old" and "new" moralities, and is the source of much of the confusion which attends that debate. The new morality in particular is often presented in attractive theoretical terms which evoke general agreement from people who react in shock when its radical implications and its frontal attack on their own unconscious legalism are spelled out in concrete illustrations.

A second reason for the order of thinking followed here is that the new morality, which is the assumed point of departure, does not prescribe the form of moral and immoral behavior *in abstracto*. The new morality is always concerned with the context in which behavior takes place and the extent to which, *in context,* behavior is consistent with a given moral ideal. This means that the new morality is bound to stating its absolutes in the most abstract theoretical terms, and then indicating what its absolute might demand or prohibit in a given situation. The preceding chapter represents an attempt to look at the given situation of contemporary American society and to identify some of the earmarks of sexual immorality from a new morality perspective. Such illustrations point to the moral absolute assumed by the new morality, but their real significance is that they give content to the discussion of theoretical issues which follows. It is hoped that the reader will read this discussion against the background provided by Chapter 2, and with that illustration in mind, fill in the content provided by his own unique experience and the ethical dilemmas with which he has been confronted.

The purpose of this chapter is to present a new morality understanding of sexual morality by (1) posing and illustrating the theoretical issues between old and new moralities, (2) establishing a Christian definition of the moral ideal invoked by the new morality, and (3) elaborating the implications of this line of thinking for an understanding of human nature.

OLD AND NEW MORALITIES

The first thing which must be said about old and new moralities is how misleading the labels are. What is often called the new morality is new only in a relative sense. As an ethical attitude, the new morality only appears to be new each time it challenges the prevailing legalism of any period or culture. It is actually very old, and has its roots firmly planted in the biblical tradition. Likewise, what is often called the old morality only appears to be old relative to the new morality. It is not at all old in the sense of being outmoded or on the decline as a popular ethical point of view. Indeed, the attitude toward the law which usually characterizes the old morality is constantly reemerging in new forms, and is a very potent force in contemporary thinking. However, it is still useful to use these terms as counters and as descriptive of a current clash of ethical attitudes which is very real.

Before describing the central issues of that clash, one important point concerning both old and new moralities needs to be reiterated. That is that neither morality is simply coterminous with a particular moral code. This is a facile equation which is often made by those who assume that the only real difference between old and new moralities is that the latter is a liberalized version of the former. That equation misrepresents both approaches because it misses the important point that each holds up the same moral code, although with radically different assumptions concerning its ultimate authority. It also misses the point that the new morality, although apparently more liberal in the forms of behavior which it entertains as potentially moral, is actually more conservative. Its apparent permissiveness is an attempt to "conserve" the biblical moral tradition against the legalism which constantly threatens it. It is also more difficult to live by and more demanding of the individual moral agent. Many do not identify these values with the word "liberal," which has come to mean free and easy. The old morality, likewise, although apparently conservative in its limitation of moral choices to certain traditional patterns, is actually more liberal. It is demonstrably easier to live by and less demanding on the individual. It may even function to adjust our concept of the good to prevailing social mores. We shall return to this paradox subsequently.

For these reasons, it is more accurate to think of the old and new moralities as ethical attitudes. That is, each represents an identifiable mind-set regarding the process of decision-making and the ways in which men may most responsibly engage in that process.

What then are the earmarks of these two attitudes? How may we distinguish them? Let us look at the issues on which these attitudes appear to differ. At least four of them are easily identifiable: (1) the relative priority of the letter versus the spirit; (2) whether the final moral authority is internal or external to man; (3) the relationship between freedom and responsibility; and (4) the relationship between moral behavior and belief.

THE LETTER VERSUS THE SPIRIT

The distinction between the letter and the spirit of the law is central to a distinction between old and new moralities. The old morality fails to draw this distinction in any significant way. The new morality is meaningless without it.

The old morality assumes that the letter and the spirit are in effect identical, and that conformity to the letter and loyalty to the spirit mean the same thing. The new morality refuses to identify the letter with the spirit and is built on the contingency that there are situations in which loyalty to the spirit of the law requires a violation of its letter. Likewise, in such situations, according to the new morality, adherence to the letter of the law for its own sake may be immoral and dehumanizing because it makes principles more important than persons. The new morality, however, does not separate the spirit from the letter of the law. It sees them as inseparable and interdependent, but not identical.

This distinction between the letter and the spirit of the law can be seen in the old morality's emphasis on the content of moral and legal commands and the new morality's emphasis on their rationale. For this reason, the old morality is often caricatured as legalism (worship of the law) and the new morality as antinomianism (opposition to the law). Both of these charges are unfair, although they point to potential abuses of old and new morality thinking. Consequently, new morality thinking which bases its arguments on opposition to legalism sets up as much of a straw man as old morality thinking which justifies itself by its opposition to anarchy. At the same time, it is fair to distinguish the old morality as primarily concerned with the content of moral codes and commandments and the new morality as primarily concerned with the reasoning behind these commandments. And where old morality thinking makes it the final moral responsibility of man to conform his behavior to the content or letter of the law, the new morality makes it his final moral responsibility to adjust his behavior to the spirit or rationale behind the commandments as he sees it in his own unique context.

Where the old morality says, "Thou shalt not steal," the new

morality counters with the question, "Why?" Where the old morality says, "Thou shalt not commit adultery," the new morality asks,
"Why?" Even when the old morality says, "Thou shalt not kill,"
the new morality is concerned to know why. And when the new
morality detects, as it does in the case of the biblical codes, a consistent rationale behind a set of commandments, it makes loyalty
and consistency with that rationale more important than conformity
to the letter of the commandments. That sounds relatively harmless
as long as it is kept in the theoretical realm. But when one points
out specific contexts in which it might be more moral and loving
to take a life, to take another man's property, or to engage in forbidden sexual practices, society becomes protective of what it sees
to be its own interests. Nowhere is this more true than with trans-
gressions of sexual taboos. Here contemporary American society
seems to be even more concerned with the letter of the law than
with the protection of private property and human life, particularly
where the property and lives are not American! The new morality is
antagonistic to such thinking. It posits the possibility of occasional
breaking of the law in the name of its spirit. It also points out that
keeping the law may on occasion be immoral and contrary to its
spirit. Thus, a "just" war or legalized business swindling is not ex-
empt from the new morality's indictments simply because it conforms to the civil or ecclesiastical code. Likewise, the legalized
exploitation of sexuality in many marriages does not escape the
questioning of a "new" moral attitude which is more concerned with
the relationship context of sexual behavior than with its conformity
to any prescribed form.

However, this tension between the letter and the spirit of the law
does not imply inevitable antagonism. If it did, the charge of antinomianism would be more justified than it is. The new morality
takes the letter of the law seriously. It does not dismiss it or
contradict it lightly. The spirit of any law requires the letter to give
it form. Without the letter, the spirit remains essentially amorphous
and therefore morally meaningless and inapplicable. The spirit is,
so to speak, read off the letter of the law. This is what Paul had in

mind when he spoke of the biblical law as a "schoolmaster" to lead men to Christ.[1] That says that the letter of the law serves to point us toward that moral ideal which is ultimate. However, the identification of the letter with that to which it points makes the letter itself ultimate. From a new morality point of view, this is a dangerous form of idolatry.

It is questionable if it is possible to set the spirit of any document over against its letter in a universal way. This is as true of the Constitution of the United States of America as it is of the biblical law. But the historical context of American life changes, and has from time to time made the letter of certain prescriptions appear unconstitutional (i.e., against the spirit of the Constitution). In the same way, the context in which the man of faith lives his life also changes. Situations develop in which the letter of the biblical law itself appears unbiblical (i.e., contrary to its own spirit).

A good illustration of new morality thinking in our time is civil disobedience, especially as it has been practiced in the interest of procuring civil rights and expressing dissent from national policies. Properly understood, civil disobedience is an expression of the highest kind of moral idealism. In the name of a higher or ultimate value, one systematically violates the letter of the civil law.[2] The law violated is usually seen as inconsistent with its own spirit, and appeal is made to that spirit in calling the law into question.

There is a difference between civil disobedience thus defined and what might be called "uncivil" disobedience. True civil disobedience demonstrates respect for the law and submission to it in the very act of violation. This usually entails the practice of nonviolence in conjunction with civil disobedience and submission to the penalties prescribed by the law. True civil disobedience is also contextual. It does not generalize about laws. Thus, for example, there is nothing particularly unjust about an ordinance concerning parade permits in a context in which that ordinance is used to keep the streets open for normal commerce. But where that ordinance is used to prevent an oppressed minority from exercising their right of assembly, it may become an appropriate target for civil disobedience. Civil disobedience is also open. It does not attempt to avoid detection, for in its openness lies its strength, both as a political stratagem and as a moral expression. This support of the law in principle while violating it in particular is what makes such disobedience civil rather than uncivil. It is a way of breaking the law which was allegedly practiced by Abraham, Socrates, and Jesus.[3] And it is both expressive and illustrative of the new morality distinction between the letter and the spirit. It also indicates how really old the new morality is.

Two Cases

1. Henry H. is a college graduate, well established in his profession, who is dating a nurse in training. After more than a year of courtship, they decide that they are in love. But the young woman has two years of nurse's training to complete, and the rules of the nursing school forbid students to marry while in course. Both people are religious, and take seriously the church's traditional taboos on premarital intercourse. But the normal course of their relationship seems to both of them to have reached the point where anything short of full sexual involvement is dishonest, frustrating, and destructive. Four basic alternatives seem open to them: (1) They can avoid intercourse and postpone their marriage until after the completion of her training. This conforms to the letter of what they understand to be the church's teaching and of the school's regulations. (2) They can marry and terminate her professional training. This also conforms to the letter of the law. (3) They can become secretly married. This conforms to the letter of social expectations but violates the letter of honesty in their relationship with her school. (4) They can sleep together without being married. This violates the letter of the social mores, but not necessarily their spirit, although it would violate the spirit of the school's regulations.

The letter versus the spirit: Where should their loyalty lie? What should they do?

What did they do? Let them tell it in their own words.

"As we tried to face the long wait, we realized that we would either break down in an incautious moment or become so frustrated that we would have to stop seeing each other. And we did not see the necessity for abstinence in the face of our devotion to each other and the fact that we would get married if the school regulations permitted it. After much discussion and prayer we decided to unite ourselves in secrecy with a pledge as binding in our hearts as any made at the altar. When nurse's training was completed we had a public ceremony affirming the same things again. We were very happy from the outset, and feel no guilt or other disturbing emotions regarding our experience. The wedding changed nothing for us except the secrecy of our relationship. We feel that secrecy is not shameful if it is undertaken in a loving cause."

Of course, no one but the two people involved can pass final judgment on the extent to which their decisions conformed to the spirit of love which they invoke. But the case clearly confronts us with the tension between the spirit and the letter.

2. Walter G.'s daughter Debbie is a young professional woman. She is carrying on a sexual affair with the graduate student with whom she feels she is in love. It is the understanding of both of them that they intend to marry as soon as it is economically feasible. In the interest of honesty in her relationship with her parents, Debbie reveals to them the nature of her relationship with her fiancé. Walter and his wife voice strong disapproval, feeling that "the intimate privileges of married life" require open acceptance of the responsibilities of marriage. The relationship continues, and some time later the couple find themselves in an economic position to marry. They approach Walter, requesting a church wedding and his blessing in the form of giving his daughter away. This places him in what he considers a moral dilemma. Can he now in honesty affirm this relationship of which he disapproves? Can he give his daughter away when she has in his eyes already given herself away? Can he participate in a church wedding which he understands to symbolize a virgin bride?

Whether or not one agrees with his presuppositions, it is clear that Walter is in an agonizing position. He is torn between what he understands to be the letter of the "law" concerning sex and marriage and the spirit of the law which values personal relationships above social institutions.

The letter versus the spirit: Where should his loyalty lie? What should he do?

What did he do?

He did everything in his power to prevent the marriage, beginning with threats of disinheritance and ending with pressures brought to bear on the clergyman involved and on the young man's family. When this failed, he refused the couple's request on both counts and publicly disavowed the marriage on the grounds of the premarital involvement. Apparently he opted for the letter of the law. He may even have reconciled spirit and letter in his own mind by believing he was acting in his daughter's best interests. Was he?

INTERNAL VERSUS EXTERNAL LOCI OF EVALUATION

The second issue on which old and new moralities differ concerns what psychologist Carl Rogers calls the "locus of evaluation" in decision-making.[4] Where does the ultimate court of appeal lie in the determination of right and wrong? From an old morality point of view, this authority is external to the individual moral agent. The court of appeal has been codified into a moral law which is assumed to be universal in its applicability. Thus, although an individual is still free to break the law for any number of reasons, it is the law itself which determines whether his behavior is right or wrong, moral or immoral.

The new morality, on the other hand, opts for what Rogers calls an *internal* locus of evaluation. This means that the final determination of right and wrong lies with the individual himself in accordance with his own highest value or moral ideal. This is why the context in which decisions are made is so important to new morality thinking. It is only when an individual takes his context seriously that he can attempt to order his behavior according to a given ideal. Actually, the internal nature of this locus of evaluation is ambiguous because an individual learns to respond to a moral ideal, such as

Love, from his environment. To this extent the moral ideal itself is externally introduced. But the new morality insists that for him to exercise real moral responsibility this ideal must be his own. He needs to have internalized it. He must be free to apply it in context as he deems most appropriate. The form of his behavior cannot be predetermined by any external code.

This emphasis on an internalizing of the locus of evaluation is central to the Sermon on the Mount, which is an appeal for an internalizing of the spirit of the Mosaic law. The recurrent refrain in the Sermon on the Mount is: "You have heard that it was said to the men of old. . . . But I say unto you . . . ." In other words, "Here is the letter of the law. But I am talking about being true to the spirit of that law, which may demand much more." For example:

> You have heard that it was said to the men of old, "You shall not kill; and whoever kills shall be liable to judgment." But I say to you that everyone who is angry with his brother shall be liable to judgment; whoever insults his brother shall be liable to the council, and whoever says, "You fool!" shall be liable to the hell of fire.[5]

And this exhortation is preceded by the admonition: "Think not that I have come to abolish the law and the prophets; I have come not to abolish them but to fulfill them."[6] In other words, life in accordance with an internalized spirit of the law is the fulfilling of the law. That is the final answer of the new morality to the charge of antinomianism. Such an understanding of morality can prompt one to pick grain on the sabbath in order to fulfill human need, in spite of explicit religious laws against such activity.[7] It is noteworthy that Rogers, from a different perspective, sees increasing health in his patients as they move from an external to an internal locus of evaluation.[8]

This emphasis on the internal dimension of decision-making focuses on the moral significance of motivation. This is consistent with a primary concern with the rationale or spirit of the law. The new morality is concerned with the reasons for which people do things. It is concerned with not only the *what* but also the *why* of behavior. It is as concerned with the spirit as with the form of behavior. The form is more important according to old morality thinking. In this, the new morality takes seriously the adage that "of all things the greatest treason is to do the right thing for the wrong reason." This is consistent with St. Paul's distinction between what is written on "cold tables of stone" and what is written in the "warm fleshiness of our hearts."[9] The former is external and *un-reason-able*. The latter is internal and clearly *reason-able,* i.e., amenable to serious questioning of its rationale. In regard to sexual behavior, this means that the final question which the new morality asks is not: "Is this form of behavior permitted or forbidden by the prescribed moral code?" but rather, "What does this form of behavior mean to me (and my partner)?" Why is this appropriate or inappropriate for us? What are our real motives? And do they tend toward the exploitation or the realization of our sexuality?

Sociologist David Riesman detects in American culture a tendency for people to become increasingly "outer-directed."[10] The forms of our behavior and the styles of our lives are determined by forces and demands external to ourselves. One of the most potent of those forces is public opinion and the expectations of others as they are molded by the mass media. Riesman is right in identifying the trend away from inner-directedness as a symptom of social sickness in our society. From a new morality perspective it is also a symptom of social immorality, a collective refusal to assume responsibility for our own lives. In the realm of sex, this outer-directedness leads to some of the sexual hypocrisies which were cited in Chapter 2, particularly the maintenance of technical virginity. One of the serious charges which the new morality brings against old morality thinking is that its emphasis on the content of the commandments fosters outer-directed decision-making and undercuts individual responsibility.

Two Cases

1. On their second date, Sheila W. is propositioned by her slightly inebriated escort. She does not find this young man particularly

attractive, feels no real affection for him, and has no desire to have intercourse with him. In terms of her internal values and motives, she is clear that she does not want to sleep with him. But she is genuinely torn by an external code (religiously grounded!) which has taught her to submit her own interests to the needs of others. She also feels the pressure of his expectations and fears alienation from him and other men if she is not more submissive sexually. And she feels some peer group pressure from college classmates who seem to find such casual sex acceptable, and who have teased her about her virginity. All of these are essentially external factors which are not a real part of Sheila's internal value structure and frame of reference. Some of them may seem transparently shallow to some readers, but they were nonetheless real external values for Sheila.

Internal versus external: What should she do? Who finally determines what is right?

What did she do?

She submitted, in a situation in which it seems clear to the outside observer that she was not being true to herself. In effect, she placed the locus of evaluation outside of herself and decided for values which were not really her own. Some might recognize in her decision-making symptoms of psychological ill-health. But the dilemma is a common one for those torn between the expectations of others and their own feelings and instincts.

2. Nancy A., a high school senior, finds herself pregnant through a relationship with a college student she intends eventually to marry. The couple are not in any way economically prepared to marry. Nancy furthermore is an outstanding student with a promising college career ahead of her. She is now confronted with a decision about her pregnancy. She can (1) marry the young man, who is willing, though reluctant, (2) deliver the child and then give it up, (3) obtain an abortion. Each alternative involves real practical risks. And each alternative is in some ways unattractive to Nancy. Alternatives 1 and 2 are legal and somewhat more acceptable according to an unwritten external code, given an unmarried pregnancy.

Alternative 3 is not only illegal, but also contrary to the religious teaching to which Nancy has been exposed. It raises questions for her about her responsibility for the life of her unborn child. But, all potential consequences considered, an abortion still seems to her the most attractive alternative and the choice most consistent with her own internal values and goals in this situation.

Internal versus external, self against the expectations of the group: What should she do? Where is the final moral authority in this decision?

What did she do?

She obtained an abortion, and now looks on the entire experience as constructive learning in the realm of decision-making. She is critical of her decision to sleep with her boyfriend, affirmative of her decision to have her pregnancy aborted. She has persuaded herself that she has made the most responsible decision regarding the life of her child—although certainly not the decision indicated by the law.

FREEDOM AND RESPONSIBILITY

The third issue in the present debate has to do with the tenuous balance between freedom and responsibility in the decision-making process. The old morality comes down very hard on the side of responsibility in this polarity. Indeed, one of the charges which it levels against the new morality is that it does not take the individual's responsibility to society, to church, and to God seriously enough, and therefore leads to lack of discipline and to license. The responsibility of which the old morality speaks is clearly a responsibility to keep the rules. According to this line of thinking, to say that an individual is responsible for his life really means that he is responsible to do what is expected of him. And what is expected of him is clearly and conveniently spelled out in the civil and moral code, to say nothing of less explicit but equally binding social mores. Thus, the responsibility of which the old morality speaks is finally responsibility to the law. It is often presented, however, as responsibility to a society, a church, or a God, and these are seen as the sources and authority of the law.

Within such a moral frame of reference there is a place for freedom, but it is a qualified and subsidiary place. Freedom itself is circumscribed by the law. It is freedom to break the law or not to break the law. It is not the freedom to break the law and be moral in doing so. This is the traditional theological freedom to sin, implied in the story of the Fall. But it is not Luther's freedom to "sin boldly," which is also implied in the Genesis myths and spelled out in the Pauline attitude toward the law.

The new morality, on the other hand, reminds us that moral responsibility implies moral freedom. I am not really responsible for my own life unless I am genuinely free in the decisions I make. *I* must determine what is right and wrong according to my own ultimate commitments. In this, the new morality takes the responsibility of the individual quite seriously. Indeed, it takes it even more seriously than the old morality. But responsibility here is understood not simply as responsibility to an external code. Responsibility here is to the object of one's ultimate commitment or faith. Responsibility here is to the highest value or moral ideal which one holds. Responsibility here is to the Spirit to which one gives his life, whether consciously or unconsciously. Within a religious frame of reference, this is responsibility to God. This is the relationship between God and the law in a new morality perspective, not that the law is God but that God is the law. And where God is defined as that total love which is revealed in Jesus of Nazareth, such a "law" can be perceived as making demands which take priority over the letter of any moral code, even those sanctified by long usage and the imprimatur of the religious establishment.

The freedom of which the new morality speaks is paradoxical. This reflects the paradoxical nature of the relationship between freedom and responsibility. New morality freedom is freedom in obedience.[11] This follows from what has been said concerning ultimate moral ideals, the sense in which God is law, and the role of faith in responsible decision-making. To speak of freedom in obedience is not to limit freedom. It is rather to realize it. Moral freedom is always exercised in a context, and one of the inevitable elements in that context is the value orientation of the individual. Freedom without this element is license. This is no freedom at all, but rather bondage to a new law, the law of license. One of the first commandments of the law of license is that under no circumstances shall you take seriously the context in which you act in order to apply some moral ideal in your decisions. Freedom in obedience means a free application in each decision of that value which is ultimately dear to one. This is freedom from the law, not freedom from God or any secular moral commitment. And it is not freedom to disregard the law, but rather freedom not to have the form of one's behavior determined by the law.

It should not be inferred from this that the new morality can only be practiced by one who is explicitly religious. It is true that the new morality has reemerged in our time on Christian soil, and has its roots deeply planted in that soil. But as an attitude the new morality can be held by any individual who is reasonably clear about what is ultimately important to him. The man of religious faith may identify such a person as a kindred spirit, but this does not mean that every new moralist needs to view himself as a man of faith.

Three Cases

1. Where freedom means bondage: Jerry T., a college sophomore, becomes aware of the extent to which his decisions are determined by the expectations of his parents and the response he anticipates from them. He determines to assert himself and embarks on a campaign of experimentation with sex, drugs, and expensive automobiles. After an unfortunate narcotics episode, paying for one abortion, a forced and unsuccessful marriage, and the loss of his financial resources he seeks out counseling help. In the early stages of counseling, he insists that in spite of the consequences of his behavior it shows that he is free and a "real" person. He does not see that the need to demonstrate freedom is itself a form of bondage. It constricts him and cuts off his resources for truly responsible freedom. The first authentically free decision he makes is probably the one to seek counseling help rather than return to submission to

his parents' expectations. Of course, this is also a responsible decision which reflects his own internal values.

2. Where responsibility means bondage: Louise K., a college-graduate professional woman, becomes pregnant through a liaison which she had regretted even before discovering her pregnancy. She does not want to marry the man and sees union with him as a mismatch, although he is willing. On the other hand, she views what she had thought was the exercise of her sexual freedom as an error, and is fearful of again contradicting the mores of her society by obtaining an abortion. Consequently, she decides to do the "responsible" thing and marry the man, even though this seems to her the wrong thing to do for all concerned.

Where is there freedom and where is there responsibility in Louise's decision? To what extent has the desire to do that which is socially accepted as responsible led her into a bondage which inhibits true freedom and true responsibility?

3. Where freedom means responsibility: Phyllis L. and Ralph P., two college students who have been courting for over a year, decide to sleep together for the last year of their engagement before marrying. After several months, it appears that the contraceptive pills Phyllis is using are having discomforting side-effects for her. However, both young people are reluctant, for a number of reasons, to experiment with other less reliable means of birth control. Consequently, they reach a new decision to refrain from intercourse until the potential pregnancy is more fully prepared for by their marriage. This decision appears to be both free and responsible. It is free because there seem to have been no coercive or compulsive factors involved, but rather a sober and realistic evaluation of potential consequences. It is probably free also because their initial decision to sleep together was freely made. It is also responsible, not because it conforms more closely to established mores, but because the decision was made *in response* to the perceived needs of the people involved.

In how many marriages do partners exercise this kind of responsibility toward one another? This kind of freedom?

MORALITY AND BELIEF

A fourth issue between the old and new moralities concerns religious commitment. This is more of a hidden agenda than the other issues cited, but it reveals important differences between the two attitudes. From an old morality perspective, morality is intimately related to some form of religious belief. This is because the law is usually viewed as the mandate of a supreme being. God gave the law, and if you want to know why you should obey it, that's why! It is correspondingly difficult for old moralists to conceive of anyone being truly moral without believing in God. According to such thinking, if you take God as a supreme law-giver out of the picture, the linchpin has been removed from the whole moral structure. Both the authority and the threat of the law have been removed. Such thinking underlies the popular myth that doctrinaire communists are immoral because they are atheists, or that atheists should not hold public office because there is no guarantee that they will behave in a moral way. The extent to which otherwise secular politicians make public bows to the religious establishment and have themselves photographed going to church is an index of how such myths still control American voting patterns.

There is irony in this assumed tie-in between religion and morality. Many people can be and are thoroughgoing old moralists without a shred of conventional religious belief or even a clear-cut ultimate commitment (except perhaps a commitment to the law itself). All that is required by the old morality is that the law be considered the final determinant of right and wrong and that one conform to it.

The new morality, on the other hand, is open to the possibility of moral behavior by the atheist as well as the theist, the agnostic as well as the believer. Belief in some kind of supreme being is not a precondition of morality, and the legal/moral code is not necessarily identified with the Deity. There is more concern with the nature of one's highest value and the ways it is expressed than with its source or the form in which it is articulated.

There is irony here too in the rejection of an indissoluble knot between morality and religion. This is because the new morality presupposes and depends on some kind of ultimate commitment. One cannot speak, for example, of the priority of the spirit over the letter of the law unless one is ultimately loyal to that spirit. One cannot speak of an internal locus of evaluation unless there is some discrete value which one has internalized and made his own. One cannot speak of the extent to which moral responsibility presupposes a radical moral freedom without also recognizing that this is freedom in obedience. But this obedience need not be viewed in a religious frame of reference or expressed in prescribed religious practices or beliefs. That is the important point. It is as possible for the humanist who is ultimately concerned for the welfare of his neighbor to behave morally as it is for the Christian who is ultimately concerned to mirror the love of Christ. Indeed, one of the key insights of the new morality is that these two commitments can mean the same thing and invoke the same spirit.

THE ETHICS OF LOVE

What such a humanist and a Christian have in common is their commitment to a person-centered ethic. They share a concern for the fulfillment of life and the personal welfare of others. This is not a sentimental concern or simply kindly feelings toward others in general. It is a radical concern for specific others. It is a concern so radical that one is willing to risk his own fulfillment for the good of another. Insofar as such a concern informs decisions, it is appropriate to speak of its expression in terms of a person-centered ethic. Such an ethic should be distinguished from a code-centered ethic which calls for keeping the rules even at the risk of failing to minister to the needs of another human being. One more distinction between old and new moralities then is the primary emphasis of the latter on a person-centered ethic.

There are various ways of defining the basic value of such an ethic. Most of them invoke an abstraction such as the self-realization of the other, self-giving, altruism, love. Rogers, who is a humanist, articulates these ethics in terms of centeredness. The central focus of one's concern is revealed in the way in which he relates to others and the kinds of decisions he makes. With Rogers's therapeutic and educational concerns, this has led to a "client-centered" approach to counseling and a "student-centered" approach to teaching.[12] Bishop John A. T. Robinson speaks for many of the neo-liberal theologians of our time when he calls such an ethic "being for others." Robinson sees Jesus, the Christian model of this ethic, as "the man for others."[13] Martin Buber speaks of the same ethic when he distinguishes between "I-Thou" and "I-It" relationships. And Buber points out that the biblical ethic comes down hard on the need for "I-Thou" relationships with the neighbor.[14] In such relationships, the neighbor is responded to as a person or subject, not used as a thing or object.

For some within the Christian neo-orthodox tradition, such ethics have been labeled "Christocentric." The focus is on Christ in terms of both being Christ to another and seeing Christ in the other.[15] This resembles the medieval concept of the *Imitatio Christi,* which is an injunction to be person-centered and loving according to the image which Jesus presents.[16] Paul is describing some of the possible expressions of a person-centered ethic in his eloquent treatise on love in the thirteenth chapter of First Corinthians. All of these differing frames of reference point to the same ethical attitude. It is that attitude which has most recently been labeled the new morality. A broad characterization of it might be "the ethics of love."

What follows is an elaboration of an explicitly biblical/Christian understanding of the ethics of love. The Christian/biblical idiom is the frame of reference of the author. It is the door through which this ethic has been revealed to him. But to elaborate a person-centered love ethic using Christian imagery does not limit this ethic to a Christian frame of reference. Neither does it ascribe any particular uniqueness to the love ethic of the Christian tradition, beyond the use of its own particular symbols and images. An elaboration of the love ethic in Christian terms simply attests to the content which that ethic can have within a Christian faith-response.

The basic norm for all ethics and questions of value in the Christian tradition is the personhood of Jesus. This is because the personhood of Jesus, the image of him revealed in the New Testament, is the basic norm for all Christian theological statements. The heart of the Christian faith-response is the confession that in Jesus is revealed the fullness of God. In him is revealed the nature of ultimate reality. This means that in him is revealed the ultimate value of life— that which ultimately defines what is right and wrong, moral and immoral. It is this spirit which is (or should be) the controlling ideal for all Christian ethics. From an explicitly Christian perspective, this spirit represents the highest moral value of the new morality.

Another way to say this is to affirm that in Jesus is revealed the fullness of the God who is Love. Or, in Jesus is revealed the fullness of Love. The man of faith who responds to Jesus as "Lord and Savior" is really saying that he responds to Jesus as *the* mediator (for him) of that which is ultimately real and important. He is saying that the image of Jesus in the New Testament is the norm for the highest value in life. Jesus gives content to the spirit to which the man of faith is obedient. Whether you want to call Christian ethics the imitation of Christ or obedience to the God revealed in Christ or following the dictates of the spirit of Christ or obedience to Christ, it all adds up to the same thing: *being person-centered in the way and to the extent that Jesus was person-centered.*

How do we know the way and the extent to which Jesus was person-centered? Clearly there is only one document, the New Testament. And that document simply tells the story of a man, embellished with a few fragmentary interpretations of his significance by those who lived shortly after him and saw themselves as his followers. Modern scholarship indicates that the picture of Jesus in the New Testament is heavily garnished with legendary and miraculous material. It is also colored by the interpretations of the Gospel writers and the limitations of the local and oral traditions available to them. But it is nonetheless the picture of a man. And it is to this picture that Christians down through the ages have responded and from which they have derived meaningful guidelines for their behavior. This is as true of those twentieth-century Christians who do not take many of the stories about Jesus to be historical fact as it is of those early Christians who did not apparently worry about the historicity of their religious mythology. It is just as true of those for whom the story has the same moral and spiritual power whether or not an historical person named Jesus ever lived.

The ethical dimension of the picture of this man is revealed in two basic ways. It is revealed in what he is alleged to have done, the style of his ministry and relationships to those around him. And it is revealed in what he is alleged to have said, the moral teachings which are gathered together in anecdotal conversations, sermonizing, and parables. This means that Christians are morally instructed by what Jesus was as well as by what he taught. And both what he was and what he taught point to a person-centered ethic. Jesus himself is the personification of the ethics of love. And that is because he is viewed as the personification of the God who is Love.

What did Jesus do that reveals a person-centered ethic? He befriended the most unattractive people of his time, those who were social outcasts — publicans, adulterers, lepers, tax collectors, even the hated Romans. This friendship was authentic and conspicuous and therefore risky. It involved intimacies like taking meals with them, being with them in ways which inevitably led to his identification with them as outcasts. This was no paternalistic slumming, according to the New Testament picture. Neither was it a kind of *noblesse oblige* social work, trying to bring a little joy into the lives of the joyless. It was instead a radical person-centered concern for others. It found its natural focus in those who seemed to be least the focus of the concern of others. It was also a concern which risked rejection and misunderstanding in the name of serving another. It was a concern which did not count the cost, because the welfare and fulfillment of another person was more important than any cost. Of course, part of the cost was an occasional breaking of the religious rules and the social taboos of Jesus's time. Anyone knew that a good

Jew did not eat with people who were unwashed, give comfort to adulterers, or consort with the hated Roman soldiers. That was tantamount to "giving aid and comfort to the enemy."[17] But breaking the rules did not seem to perplex Jesus, who appeared unusually clear as to where his ultimate loyalties lay. They lay with the biblical God, the author and spirit of the Mosaic Law, the power of Love.

On the sabbath, when religious taboos forbade such work, the same Jesus engaged in such person-centered acts as healing and picking grain to fill empty stomachs.[18] And when reprimanded for this lawlessness, he scolded his accusers for being blind to the meaning of a person-centered ethic and untrue to the tradition which they espoused. Anyone knows that you don't wait until tomorrow to save a lost sheep or a drowning man. And even the great King David did not let the letter of the law interfere with his fulfilling its spirit vis-à-vis basic human needs.

Likewise, when a jar of costly ointment was apparently wasted in a ritual act, the moralists among Jesus's own band were offended. The law would appear to have been better kept by selling the ointment and giving the proceeds to the poor. But Jesus responded in a way which continues to surprise even the contemporary reader. His response was one of concern for the individual involved. He recognized the person-centered significance of the act in its context.[19]

Illustrations of this dimension of Jesus's style of life abound. All that he did and was points, however, to the one act which has continued to be the central symbol of his love. This is giving up his life in devotion to his ideal/God. Its symbol is the Cross. The Cross symbolizes the ultimate criterion of the Christian ethic because it portrays graphically the magnitude of the concern which the gospel proclaims. The Cross is the measure of the extent to which person-centeredness goes if it is authentic. It goes about as far as it can go. It goes to the giving up of one's self. It is the Cross which makes Christian love total love rather than a pale or sentimental imitation. And it is the Cross which makes the Christian ethic so radically idealistic. One need not talk in Crucifixion terms in order for his ideal to be total self-giving. But if he does talk in Crucifixion terms, that ideal should be nothing less than total self-giving. The Cross defines the ultimate value of the Christian ethic in terms of a willingness to risk one's own destruction for the sake of one or more others. It is through the Cross, more than through any other one act, that Jesus becomes the norm for Christian ethics. His prior ministry, of course, gives a special content to the Cross. But the Cross casts his prior ministry in an entirely new perspective. In a real sense, the symbol of the Cross includes all that Jesus was or did.

The "good news" of the Christian proclamation is that the Cross is not the end of the story. The good news is that through total self-giving comes total self-realization. The good news is that while you can kill Jesus, you can't kill the spirit revealed in him. The good news is that because he died the fullness of that spirit (Love) can be revealed to us so that it may govern our lives. "For all who are led by the Spirit of God are sons of God."[20] And, as Paul recognized, with that governance, with that gift, with that power, comes freedom from the law. In this sense, the Cross quite literally marks the birth of a new morality.

This is what Jesus was and did. What he taught was an exhortation to what he did. He taught, for example, that "inasmuch as ye do it unto one of the least of these, ye do it unto me."[21] That says that service of the neighbor's needs is service of Christ. It is an exhortation to make all decisions on a person-centered basis and to strive to see Christ in the person of another. In the parable of the sheep and the goats which precedes that saying, the lesson is that the truly righteous are those who feed the hungry, give drink to the thirsty, welcome the stranger, clothe the naked, visit the sick and imprisoned. What are these but person-centered acts which reflect the ethics of love?

When Jesus was asked what one must do to inherit eternal life (i.e., to participate now in that which is eternal), he cited the commandments, but then illustrated what they mean by telling the parable of the Good Samaritan.[22] The "goodness" of the Samaritan is his aid of a fellow human being in need. His act, which sets no preconditions on his benevolence and asks for no rewards, is good because it reflects the spirit of the Mosaic Law. And he is a Samaritan, not even necessarily a religious person, let alone a Jew living under the Mosaic Law.

Jesus also used a shepherd image to refer to himself. This dramatizes the dimension of care and personal concern for his fellow man which is the key to his ministry. [23] The shepherd image symbolizes the person-centered nature of any ethic which would pattern itself after his ministry.

In the same vein, Jesus used the image of the servant to describe the highest expression of human life (greatness in the kingdom of God). And he explicitly exhorted his disciples to be servants of one another.[24] A servant is, of course, one whose actions are keyed on the needs of other human beings. Indeed, the servant motif is central to Jesus's self-understanding and to a proper understanding of the vocation of the church. This motif is taken from the Old Testament where Israel is called to understand herself as a servant people. It reaches its highest expression in Isaiah 40–55,[25] from which Jesus probably derived his understanding of his own vocation as a "suffering servant." The addition of the dimension of suffering to service is simply the fulfillment of the service of the neighbor. It points up the extent to which the person-centeredness of the man of faith will go. The concept of *suffering* service introduces the Crucifixion into our understanding of Christian vocation and the Christian ethic. It points to the sense in which person-centeredness is the opposite of self-centeredness.

Jesus's teaching also will not limit morality to particular religious practices or beliefs. Not all of the people who call Jesus "Lord" will populate the kingdom of heaven.[26] The final test will instead be doing "the will of my Father which is in heaven." And this is in a context in which the "will of my Father" has just been spelled out in terms of the spirit rather than the letter of the law.

Jesus reportedly taught that man was not made for the sabbath, but the sabbath for man.[27] That is an assertion of a person-centered attitude which sees human beings as more important than any principle, institution, custom, or code.

Perhaps most important of all, Jesus taught that he who would find his life must first lose it.[28] The Gospels are filled with references to this paradox of the Christian style of life. It means that service of the neighbor takes priority over all other considerations, including the preservation of one's own life. Like the suffering servant motif, this is a foreshadowing of the Crucifixion. More than anything else, this teaching of Jesus should make it clear that concern for the neighbor is to be the ultimate value in every decision. At the very heart of the ethics of love is the willingness and the desire to give up one's own life, welfare, prerogatives, interests, possessions for the good of another.

What then are the implications of such teaching for sexual decisions? Certainly the ethics of love do not mean that "love makes it right," as Richard Hettlinger puts it in his book on sex and the college student.[29] Hettlinger rightly points out that this justification of sexual practices simply does not hold water from a Christian perspective, at least not until one has defined what he means by love. Where that definition is overly romanticized (where it ignores the Crucifixion and the totally-for-the-other dimension in the biblical understanding of love), it is a poor measure of whether sexuality is being realized rather than exploited. Most popular definitions of love are far removed from the biblical understanding. They are more akin to a combination of fantasy thinking and glandular excitation than to any real depth of human relationship. That is why they are popular. They are not demanding. They generally exclude the dimension of self-giving, in which, according to the biblical view, is found true self-receiving. Self-receiving in sex is the realization of one's personhood through the realization of one's sexuality. This biblical understanding of love is so eminently unpopular that it has been rather infrequently practiced, and even those who espouse it regularly confess their inability to live up to it.

Love then, in the proper biblical understanding, does make anything "all right." But none of the garden variety of popular surrogates for love carries justifying power in the moral court of appeal to which the Christian ethic points.

This, however, is not all that a Christian person-centered ethic has to say in the realm of sexual behavior. Because the self-giving defined by Jesus is the ultimate moral value, no code, taboo, or custom can be the final court of appeal in questions of sexual morality. All codes can be realistically viewed as culturally and historically conditioned. Mores are always relative, never absolute in and of themselves. In the historical and cultural context which produced them they may reflect a very high expression of the spirit of the love ethic. But they are not coterminous with that spirit because they are not eternal as the spirit is. This means that the indictments which a code brings in against certain sexual practices may be off base. It also means that forms of sexual self-expression which the code condones may in some contexts be immoral. For example, homosexuality and masturbation in some contexts may be moral. Intercourse in marriage is in some situations immoral.

Secondly, a person-centered morality cannot spell out the conditions under which behavior forbidden by the prevailing code might be morally commendable. Such efforts are not only misleading and necessarily fragmentary. They also reduce morality to casuistry. And casuistry is generally little more than a refined and sophisticated legalism. It is an attempt to purify the ambiguities of the law by spelling out the specific conditions under which certain violations of the law might be consistent with the spirit of the law. Casuists are usually on the right track in focusing on the priority of the spirit, and on the wrong track in trying to spell that priority out in a new letter. In spite of the fact that it has been called "neo-casuistry" by some,[30] there is no place in new morality thinking for formal casuistry. Nowhere is this more clear than in the controversial realm of premarital intercourse, where new morality proponents are constantly badgered to spell out the conditions under which this sexual act can be condoned. To do this would be simply to proclaim a new and more liberal law. And such a law itself would become the focus of the same kind of idolatries and legalism which have attended the old law for some time. A new law is precisely what the new morality is not and was never intended to be.

Is the new morality's offering in the sexual realm then simply pious phrases about biblical love without attempts to give those phrases any contextual content? No. The new moralist as a counselor is called to join the struggle with every individual who is attempting to come to grips with his sexuality and to find appropriate modes for its expression. That struggle will be more difficult and agonizing than citing either an old or a new law to him. But then, the new morality is always harder than the old morality. This struggle will often be marked by a painstaking examination of the context of an individual's life and relationships. It will be marked by a sometimes frustrating search with him for his real values. It will be marked by a searching out of potential personal implications of his sexual behavior. It will be marked by an examination of all those relationships in which a person-centered morality may bear on his sexual decision-making. It will involve raising thorny questions concerning an individual's view of his own sexuality and the meaning of the sexual act to him. In the realm of premarital intercourse, this struggle with and on behalf of another may involve uncomfortable confrontations with specific moral responsibilities. What about responsibility to one's sexual partner? To a potential child? To parents and others more or less directly involved? Even to other lovers — past, present, and future?

All of these factors, and many others, go to make up the context in which one makes a decision. They are never raised by the new moralist as moral thumbscrews in an effort to persuade an individual to follow one or another course of action. They are raised because the new morality is so thoroughly contextual in its orientation. They are raised because this is the only way that any authentic new moralist goes about making his own decisions — in sex as in everything else. In the end, it is important that the individual be as free as possible to make his own decisions, in accordance with what he sees as his own highest value. Otherwise, the new morality would not be very new, even in a relative sense. Otherwise, the other person might be deprived of an opportunity to realize his own full humanity as a decision-maker. Such a willful deprivation could be a serious violation of a person-centered ethic.

AN OPTIMISTIC DOCTRINE OF MAN

It should be clear that the new morality presupposes an optimistic doctrine of man. The new morality is optimistic about the human potential to make moral decisions. This means that the new morality is optimistic about the capacity of human nature for self-giving love.

This may seem strange in light of the man of faith's awareness of how frequently he fails to live up to his ideal. But there is an important difference between failure to realize a capacity and gross incapacity, no matter what the frequency of failure. The new morality posits the human capacity to act in a self-satisfying and self-giving way, and builds its whole ethic on this capacity. The invoking of love as an ultimate value does not make sense if you do not believe that it is realizable. It makes no more sense if you believe that it was realizable for only one human being, the Sinless One, and that all the rest are therefore chained to the law by their sins. Such thinking not only rings the death knell for person-centered ethics by assuming they are impossible. It also makes Jesus a superman who is something more or less than fully human. And it leads to a moral cynicism which is incapable of celebrating the gift of love at the heart of the Christian affirmation.

To say that the new morality is optimistic about human nature is not to say that its view is pollyanna. A pollyanna view is one which does not jibe with the facts of human experience. It is not realistic. Or, as some critics of the new morality put it, it does not take sin seriously.

But new moralists tend to think that they are taking sin very seriously. Their doctrine of man seems to them realistic because it jibes with their own experience of themselves as both lovers and sinners. Indeed, one charge against old morality thinking is that it is unrealistic because it does not take seriously enough the "God-given" human capacity to love.

Part of the problem here is that new and old moralists tend to mean different things by sin. Within an old morality frame of reference, sin is most frequently understood as the breaking of the law. Sin, like righteousness, is defined by the law. But according to the new morality, sin is the exact opposite of the ultimate value of love. Sin is un-love. Sin is refusing to be for the other. Sin is disobedience, not of the law, but of the supreme Love which is also God. Sin is therefore a theological category. This is consistent with the biblical understanding, where sin is seen in relationship to the Deity and portrayed mythologically in terms of disobedience of the Deity. Where sin is thus understood, it becomes more appropriate to speak of one's *sin* than one's *sins*. *Sin* is the human propensity to be unloving, while *sins* often simply refer to violations of a given code. Of course, the new moralist is aware of specific sins on his part. But these represent occasions on which he sees himself as unloving, rather than categorical acts which contradict the prescribed mores.

To the charge that its view of man is pollyanna, the new morality answers that it takes sin seriously, but only because it first takes seriously its opposite and defining number—Love. Where love is established as the ultimate moral ideal, sin is recognized as the human condition which makes us needful and aware of such an ideal. Where man's capacity to love is assumed, his capacity not to love is implied. Indeed, logically, love is meaningless as a concept unless it is understood as freely offered. Enforced self-giving is immediately something less than total self-giving. And for love to be truly free, its opposite, un-love, must be at least a live option. The same argument holds in reverse, moving from sin to love, although those who want to base their ethics on a doctrine of sin ignore this point. What is at issue here is the central biblical paradox of moral freedom. It is not unrelated to the paradox of freedom and responsibility of which the new morality makes so much.

The new moralist, therefore, is aware of the human propensity to be unloving. But he takes this seriously only as one factor in the experiential context in which he makes his decisions. He does not use it as an excuse to abdicate his moral responsibility to any code. Neither does he take it as a mandate to prevent other people from making real moral choices simply because they might not make the most loving choice. Since these are the ways in which the old moralist takes sin seriously, it is not surprising that he usually thinks that the new moralist does not take it seriously at all.

A meaningful distinction, consequently, may be drawn between an ethic based on sin and an ethic based on love. An ethic based on sin is one which sees the task of morality as the controlling of unruly human passions, protecting man from himself and from his neighbor.[31] Most civil laws reflect such an aim, and appropriately so. But, according to the new morality, civil laws are not the basis of morality. At their best they may be expressions in context of a particular moral spirit. But their codification is always a concession to the unloving tendencies of human nature. Such laws do not hold out a moral challenge or ideal to man. They simply exercise some social restraint on his tendencies to be immoral. This is what St. Paul has in mind when he identifies the law with sin and vice versa.[32] He is saying that the need for laws is a symptom of our human sickness. They are given to us, as Jesus put it, "for the hardness of our hearts."[33] But that does not make the law in any way supreme. Neither does it make it a basis for morality.

The only real basis for morality, according to the new morality, is the ideal of love. An ethic based on love holds out a moral challenge and ideal to man rather than legal restrictions. It appeals to his potential for love rather than un-love, although it does not ignore the latter. The task of any morality, according to such a view, is the evoking of the highest in human self-expression rather than the controlling of the lowest. No law can enforce an ethic based on love, although some laws can reflect it vis-à-vis a particular cultural and historical milieu. Even those laws, however, may need to be violated in the name of the love ideal when one's specific context is not consistent with the general context for which they were framed. An ethic based on the capacity to love might then be called a "positive" ethic, as opposed to the negativism of an ethic based on sin. It is also an optimistic ethic, as opposed to the essential pessimism and fear of sin which informs much legalism and old morality thinking.

What are the implications of such an optimistic doctrine of man for decisions specifically in the sexual sphere? There are at least three which seem rather clear-cut.

One is that optimism about man means optimism about his sexuality. If sexual differentiation is central to human nature, then an optimistic view of human nature implies optimism about human sexuality and its potential. One's sexuality can then never be viewed primarily as a threat, a dangerous dimension of human existence to be carefully controlled. On the contrary, sexuality will be viewed as a symbol of man's highest potential, his potential for self-realization and the realization of another in self-giving. Like all valid symbols, this symbol participates in that to which it points. Sex is a medium of self-actualization and a potential vehicle of the highest expression of a truly person-centered morality. This view does not yield any easy answers to decisions regarding one's sexuality. But it sets a context in which such decisions may be made freely, joyfully, and realistically, rather than in a constricted, fearful, and unrealistic way.

Second, an optimistic doctrine of man means that one learns sexual responsibility by being given it. That means, of course, being granted genuine moral freedom to make one's own decisions in this realm. This freedom does not entail withholding guidelines or ideals. It simply requires that the final decision is up to the individual who has been exposed to the guidelines, and (what is more important) confronted with the ideal. There is a tragic irony in the assumption by some that freedom in the sexual realm is actually theirs to give and that it can be withheld by invoking the law ever more loudly, particularly in the ears of unmarried, sexually eligible young adults.

This is especially clear in the anachronism of proprietary rules for college women. Any sexually capable young adult knows that he or she is already free in this realm. What most need and long for is not attempts to control their freedom but the proclamation of reasonable ideals and guidelines for the responsible use of that freedom. Proprietary rules proclaim neither ideals nor reasonable guidelines. They do not even communicate the concern of the institution for the individual, with which they are often buttressed. And students who use them as a moral yardstick or to abdicate their own responsibility are not learning to be responsible citizens. One thinks particularly of the girl who says that dormitory closing hours provide a convenient excuse for saying "No" or terminating an unhappy date.

What proprietary rules do communicate is disrespect for the individual. But in order to evoke morally responsible behavior one must demonstrate respect for the capacity of the individual to make responsible decisions. Such respect is a natural earmark of an optimistic doctrine of man. One who holds such a view will communicate respect for the moral potential of others. Likewise, one who does not hold such a view cannot conceal his lack of respect for the moral capacities of another, even if he tries to cloak it under the facade of liberal language and apparently liberal thinking. This is particularly true of those who try to use the new morality in a manipulative way. They proclaim it in order to talk people into keeping the same old rules. A parent once told the author that she supported his views because she found them the most effective way to keep her daughter out of bed with her boyfriend. Authentic new morality thinking respects the moral freedom of the individual too much to engage in such spurious strong-arm tactics. This means, however, that the new morality entails an element of risk. The individual, after all, may decide to act in an unloving way. The new morality entertains this risk as a live option.

This riskiness is a third implication of an optimistic doctrine of man for sexual decisions. It is actually not avoided by old morality thinking, in spite of its pretensions to the contrary. The only difference between the two attitudes on this point is that the new morality acknowledges and celebrates risk as part of genuine moral freedom and responsibility. The old morality mistakenly believes that it has minimized risk by elevating the law or making it more stringent. A more positive view of the risk of moral error also influences the ways in which one views errors in retrospect, particularly in the sexual realm. We have seen that the new moralist views his sin (moral error) as a symptom of his humanness, a propensity to be unloving. Past sins (occasions on which one has acted in an unloving way) are to be appropriately repented, where repentance includes a determination to be more loving in the future. But sins are not viewed as ineradicable. Most important, their "sting" has been removed. They do not have the power to paralyze one's capacity for future decisions out of fear of making another error. This view of the risk of moral error is at the heart of the Christian understanding of forgiveness and its power. It also underlies Luther's dictum to sin boldly, and Paul's understanding that the man of faith has been delivered from the power of sin.[34]

In the sexual realm, this means that what are politely called "past indiscretions" (what here might be called former exploitations of sexuality) do not leave an ineradicable tinge on one's person or one's sexuality. The only thing eternal ·about sexual involvement is its communication of that which alone is eternal—Love. There can no more be eternal damnation for sin in the sexual sphere than for sin in any sphere. The risk of exploitation is welcomed in the new morality's call for moral freedom. And a preoccupation with past errors is seen as paralyzing future sexual fulfillment. This makes such preoccupation itself exploitative and immoral.

This point flies in the face of some of the idolatries encouraged by the cult of the virgin. It means that the loss of one's virginity in a premarital sexual encounter is *not* the most morally debilitating thing that can happen to an individual. It does not need to leave an ineradicable emotional scar. The scars are usually the result of the wounds inflicted by a sexually hypocritical society on a morally sensitive individual. And the moral issue in premarital sexual behavior, as in all sexual behavior, is not the loss of virginity but the extent to which sexuality is exploited or realized.

An optimistic doctrine of man which takes an optimistic view of sexuality, and which· identifies the teaching of responsibility with giving it, will not be preoccupied with what, morally speaking, are nonessentials.

CONCLUSION: GUIDELINES?

Some may still want to ask: But what does the new morality say specifically about how I ought to conduct my sex life? What should I do, and what shouldn't I do? How far should I go?

To such questions, one can only repeat what has been said before.

"All" that the new morality says is that you should conduct your sex life *lovingly*. Where new morality thinking has a Christian basis, what *lovingly* means will be illustrated with reference to Jesus. Beyond this, the new morality will not prescribe what you should and should not do. Neither will it tell you how far you should go. That is because such decisions can only be made in the context of particular relationships. If they are made for you by some external authority, or if they are made by you in advance in a way that is non-contextual,[35] they will not really be your decisions. They will not represent the invocation of *your* ideal in *your* involvement. They will not be truly free decisions. And consequently they will not be moral.

4

sex and marriage

THE CHURCH HAS traditionally identified heterosexual union with marriage. This institution represents society's attempt to identify and prescribe the conditions under which intercourse is acceptable. It reflects a need for social controls on the sexual drive in order to minimize its expression in ways threatening to the social order. Where marriage is understood in a monogamous way, a particular culture is saying that limitation to one sexual partner is the least socially threatening and the most socially rewarding framework for the expression of the sexual drive.

That the church has affirmed a monogamous sexual arrangement and buttressed it with religious taboos does not mean that there is anything eternal or God-given about such an arrangement. The church as religious establishment is simply doing here what the church generally does vis-à-vis social mores. It is affirming the status quo, the already-agreed-upon social arrangement. The church's traditional way of affirming is to baptize and to bless. When the church baptized the institution of marriage, it took it into itself and assumed responsibility for it. When the church blessed the institution of marriage, it elevated it to a status where it accrued a religious mystique and came to be understood as a sacrament. This is not inappropriate since marriage can represent the meeting of two human beings in a context marked by mutual responsibility and interdependence. It can represent the ultimate expression of genuinely person-centered self-giving. But when the church's baptism and blessing of marriage mean exclusive ecclesiastical control over the institution (as it did in medieval times) or veneration for the institution beyond the relationship it symbolizes (as it does today), this development is both inappropriate and idolatrous. It is inappropriate because it is presumptuous and self-defeating for the religious establishment to assume secular authority qua establishment. It is idolatrous because a man-made institution is elevated to ultimate status, a symbol takes priority over that to which it points, and the essentially conditioned is worshipped in place of the unconditional (Love).

A more relativistic view of marriage places it theologically and morally under the rubric of the law. One can say of the institution of marriage what Jesus reportedly said of institutionalized divorce, notably that it is given to us "for the hardness of our hearts." The function of the institution itself, including its vows and taboos, is socially defensive—just like the function of the law. This does not mean that marriage cannot have potent symbolic power. Nor does it mean that marriage cannot point to and participate in the ultimate expression of human love. It does not mean that marriage cannot have sacramental significance. Marriage can and does have all this, even in our time. Just as the letter of the law functions as an outward and visible sign (sacrament) of its spirit, so the institution of marriage can function as an outward and visible sign of the fulfillment of human beings in one another. However, this does not justify the imposition of this institution on an alien culture or in an alien context within one's own culture. A particular sexual arrangement which is identified with marriage is as relative to the cultural context which produces it as is a particular law. It should also be as amenable to violation in the name of its own spirit as the letter of the biblical law is amenable to violation in the name of its spirit (God).

However, the church's traditional understanding of marriage still has much to teach us concerning the nature of sexual morality. If the contemporary church would listen to its own understanding of marriage in regard to sex, morality, and responsibility instead of trying to rigidify and codify it, both the divorce rate and the number of unions uncritically blessed by the church might be significantly reduced.

What follows is a discussion of the relationship between heterosexual union and marriage, under the headings of (1) a covenant understanding of marriage, (2) the meaning and morality of sex within the covenant, and (3) the meaning and morality of sex outside the covenant. It is an attempt to avail ourselves of the traditional Christian understanding of marriage as a moral teacher without elevating it into a moral absolute.

MARRIAGE AS COVENANT

Within the Christian tradition, the most popular analogue for the marriage relationship has been the covenant. This image is taken from Scripture, where it is used to describe the relationship between the Deity and his people.[1] The early church borrowed this image from its Jewish heritage, although the image has never been as widely applied to marriage within Judaism as within Christianity.[2]

A covenant is a contract between two parties who bind themselves together with the promise of certain reciprocal services. This is the understanding in the Old Testament, where the normative covenant is made between the Lord and the people of Israel in the Exodus.[3] Through what is perceived as his saving act, the Lord promises to be their God, and the people of Israel promise to be his people. Among other things, this entails the promise to obey his commandments. In effect, mutual and reciprocal services are vowed, although it is clear that this does not necessarily imply equality between the two parties.[4]

The duration of such a covenant is indefinite. However, in intention the covenant is eternal and the two parties understand themselves to be bound to each other forever. The possibility is nevertheless entertained that the covenant may be abrogated by either party's failing to keep its part of the bargain. One of the recurrent motifs in Israel's history is her amazement that the Lord has remained steadfastly loyal to the covenant in spite of her faithlessness and disobedience.[5] This points to the sense in which the biblical understanding of love extends beyond the letter of any law or contract. The love of God is understood to be a covenant love. But it is understood to be so totally self-giving that it perseveres even where the conditions of the covenant are violated. It is so powerful that it survives even where the covenant is rejected.

The same understanding of love is assumed as the model for each partner in Christian marriage. This is why marriage can be viewed in the Christian tradition as a covenant relationship. In this covenant the ideal love is seen as transcending the conditions of any covenant, just as in the biblical drama. This is consistent with viewing marriage as an institution under the rubric of the law. Even though the covenant itself is freely given and freely responded to, in the making of a covenant one binds himself in a way that puts him under the law. Throughout the biblical tradition one cannot speak of covenant without also speaking of law, although in the New Testament an attempt is made to de-literalize this law.

Where the covenant image is used for the marriage relationship, three discrete criteria for marriage emerge. These are (1) the mutual consent of the two parties, (2) the assent of the social order, and (3) the lifelong intention of their relationship. Insofar as marriage signifies a full heterosexual relationship, these criteria are also ascribed to heterosexual union. What a covenant understanding says about marriage it also says about sexual union. This means that a covenant view of marriage sees sex as involving private consent, public assent, and lifelong intention.

Let us examine each of these dimensions, with a special view to their implications for sexual morality.

MUTUAL CONSENT

That marriage involves the mutual consent of two parties seems self-evident, although this dimension of the marriage covenant has often been ignored, even within the church. To make such consent an earmark of full heterosexual relationships is, of course, to take seriously the subjectivity of the persons involved. It is to recognize that neither can responsibly engage in a real relationship unless his "engagement" is freely given. What is frequently overlooked is the moral implication of such a view of marriage when it is applied to intercourse, within or outside of marriage. If marriage is not complete without mutual consent, so also sexual intercourse is not complete (fully realized, proper, moral) without mutual consent. Such a view of the morality of intercourse is as binding on those who are married as it is on those who are not. It reflects person-centered concern as an ultimate value, and refuses to give its moral imprimatur to any act or attitude which does not take another person's subjectivity and moral freedom completely seriously.[6] Under such a view, any sexual act which is exploitative, manipulative, or coercive of another person falls under moral indictment, whether or not it takes place within the bonds of matrimony.

Most married people know that sexual exploitation, manipulation, and even coercion can be common fare in marriage. They are certainly not necessarily excluded by the tying of the marriage knot. And manipulation and coercion need not be blatant in order to be exploitative and morally questionable. They are usually subtle, invoking all of the lethal emotional weapons at one's disposal, including guilt, shame, and fears of inadequacy.

Likewise, in sexual relations outside marriage, those who justify their behavior on grounds of consent may need to ask themselves the same questions concerning the subtle, manipulative dimensions of their sex lives. What choices are really open to oneself and one's partner? What consequences for the relationship and the individual are explicitly or implicitly ascribed to these choices? To what extent is a sense of duty (to either the law of sexual freedom or the law of sexual non-freedom!) a factor in one's decision-making?

These questions are raised by a view of marriage which stresses mutual consent in full heterosexual relationships. They are illustrative of the extent to which a covenant view of marriage implies a sexual morality transcending the limits of any particular marital arrangement. This is a sexual morality which also transcends marriage itself, and applies to the unmarried as well as the married.

George and Sally P. have been married eleven years and have three children when they come seeking counseling help. The immediate crisis is that Sally has discovered that George is sleeping with his secretary. They decide to seek counseling in an effort to save their marriage "for the children's sake," perhaps the first major decision on which they have reached authentic mutual consent. What unfolds is a long history of sexual coercion, manipulation, and dishonesty. They were first married under the pressure of a false pregnancy. George still feels he was tricked. On the other hand, Sally feels she was "talked into" sleeping with George before they were married on the basis of fraudulent promises. Shortly after the birth of their first child, it appears that George became sexually disinterested and Sally forced his attentions by threatening him with infidelity. After this, George came to feel that he could only perform sexually with his wife after several drinks. She in turn felt used and resisted this, although he was often able to force sexual relations under these circumstances.

Here apparently is a series of violations of the covenant dimension of mutual consent, both in their sex life and in the making of the marriage contract. Significantly, George feels the relationship with his secretary is the first authentic sexual relationship he has had; but the secretary subsequently breaks off the relationship when she comes to feel that she is manipulating George. Both within and outside the marriage, mutual consent has been experienced here as a powerful moral and psychological criterion of authentic sexual relations.

PUBLIC ASSENT

A second dimension of a covenant marriage is public assent, the formal affirmation of a relationship by the community or its designated representatives. This aspect of the covenant is not as clear in the biblical model as the dimensions of consent and lifelong intention. Witnesses were not necessary, for example, for God's covenant with Israel to "take." But, according to the biblical view, the making of a covenant itself is a corporate act. Even where the covenant seems individualistic (as, for example, with Noah and Abraham)[7] the individual is functioning as a corporate personality, a representative of a greater community—in the case of Noah, mankind, in the case of Abraham, Israel. Where the covenant represents a corporate decision, the community itself is a company of witnesses and public assent is included. There is a sense in which each Israelite affirms the covenant which his brother makes with the God of Israel. This covenant then is not secret. It is open, publicly acknowledged, and publicly affirmed. In the Old Testament, it is even periodically renewed publicly.[8]

The need for public assent to the marriage covenant underlies the legal requirement for witnesses at a wedding. For the same reason, a "church marriage" represents the affirmation (blessing) of a union by the religious community. This betokens recognition that every heterosexual relationship has social implications beyond itself. Just as "no man is an island," so also no twosome can be an island. For one thing, every heterosexual union is potentially reproductive. It has the potential to add a new human life to the community. For another, every deep heterosexual relationship has implications for one's other relationships. Thus, establishment of a sexual union which involves mutual consent and a dimension of lifelongness cannot help but influence the relationships two people will establish with others. The posture of each partner vis-à-vis the social order is altered by a full heterosexual relationship. Therefore, the community sees itself as having a stake in this covenant, and emphasizes the need for its assent. This underscores the socially defensive function of the marriage institution itself.

What are the moral implications when this view of marriage is applied to intercourse, within or outside of marriage? What are its implications for a viable sexual morality? First, it means that heterosexual union need not and should not be concealed from the community within which it takes place. There is nothing surreptitious about a genuine sexual relationship. Its glories should be publicly celebrated and its responsibilties should be publicly assumed. Of course, where the community is judgmental toward authentic relationships outside marriage, real covenants may be forced underground to avoid social stigma. It is difficult to be public about one's sexual covenant where arbitrary conditions have been set for an acceptable covenant. But this is already a distortion of a covenant view. It is not justified by the establishment of public assent as an earmark of sexual union.

Hence, intercourse not publicly acknowledged is lacking in something. For example, it is lacking in a public assumption of the responsibilities of sexual relations. This includes the responsibility for potential offspring and the responsibility of the partners to one another and for one another's welfare. All of this is spelled out in most formal religious marriage vows. But we have so romanticized wedding ceremonies that these vows are usually not taken very seriously by either the participants or the witnesses, to say nothing of the officiating clergyman. Of course, these responsibilities can be assumed conscientiously in private. They often are. Many young couples, both married and unmarried, have privately agreed that they are to all intents and purposes married before consummating their relationship in intercourse. That they feel it necessary to go through such charades indicates their presentiment of the interpersonal dimension of intercourse. It also indicates the hypocrisy of a society which craves genuine sexual involvement but refuses to recognize it without preconditions. The burden of moral proof in concealed heterosexual union lies with the participants as to why they are unwilling to make a public acknowledgement of their relationship and its responsibilities. But it also lies with the social order as to why it is unwilling to accept such an acknowledgement outside of a very limited and preconceived context. Of course, this burden weighs as much on the married as on the unmarried. We forget this when we romanticize marriage to the point where it has practically nothing to do with sex. This has reached the extreme of removing all references to sex from the marriage service.[9] But the marriage service is, among other things, still a public announcement that two people are going to bed together!

Some people who engage in unmarried intercourse feel, with some justification, that they have made a genuine public announcement of their relationship. For example, within a peer group or community of common commitment, some young people do openly acknowledge their relationship. They feel that within the community of common values in which they move they have procured public assent to their covenant. Within such a sub-community (for example, students working together for civil rights) the integrity of their union will usually be vigorously defended. Such people often perceive themselves as deeply alienated from the larger community of which they are (however unwillingly) a part. This includes alienation from what are viewed as the hypocritical values of the social order and some of its more constrictive assumptions concerning human sexuality. If there is error in this kind of redefinition of public assent vis-à-vis sexual union, it is the failure to recognize that for good or ill one is still a member of the larger social order. And sub-communities which define themselves against the larger community are generally emotionally, economically, and ideologically dependent on the social order in which they find themselves. It is a tragedy of our time that when the idealistic sub-community fails to recognize its relationship to the larger community it aggravates their mutual alienation. This is tragic because in America the larger community is in such drastic need of moral idealism.

Steven R., a divorced college professor in his early thirties, seeks counseling help over a current affair with a young professional woman, Wilma W. Although Steven and Wilma have justified their affair to themselves in sophisticated intellectual terms, Steven experiences what are for him unexplained pangs of remorse. At the time he seeks help, these feelings are beginning to take their toll on the harmony of the relationship, and Steven is anxious not to lose something which he considers authentic. On the other hand, his prior marital experience makes him extremely reluctant to formalize the relationship. Although publicly discreet, Steven and Wilma move in rather *avant-garde* intellectual circles in which their relationship is recognized for what it is and for the most part is accepted at face value. To his knowledge, Steven is not disturbed by any public disapproval of his behavior. He has shared his concerns with Wilma, who is sympathetic, but does not share his feelings. For her part, Wilma feels ready to marry Steven, but is in no hurry, and will not do so until she is persuaded Steven is ready to undertake the commitment wholeheartedly. She sees herself as helping him learn that their relationship is and can be real.

What then is the source of Steven's guilt feelings? Something in his prior marriage? The sense that he is using Wilma as long as he will not marry her? Perhaps. But he reached a different conclusion about himself. He decided that he could not tolerate the secretiveness of the relationship, in spite of its rather open acceptance within his subcommunity. He came to feel that until he could publicly and openly assume responsibility for Wilma and their relationship, he could not continue it. Significantly, at this point he felt free to make a decision about her. And he decided to terminate the relationship, since he was certain that he was not ready to marry. It appears that his very strong intellectual justifications had shielded him from some of his own deeper feelings regarding the dimension of public assent in a full sexual relationship.

Of course, this illustration proves nothing concerning the covenant understanding of public assent. But it indicates how deeply embedded this dimension can be in an individual's moral sensibilities.

LIFELONG INTENTION

A third dimension of a covenant understanding of marriage is lifelong intention. This is explicitly acknowledged in most Christian marriage services, and is reflected in canons regarding divorce and remarriage within Roman Catholicism. A covenant is lifelong in intention because anything less would also be less than a covenant. One does not bind oneself to mutual responsibility and interdependence with another person "for the next ten years," "for a two-year trial period and then we'll renew the contract if it works," "for better but not for worse." This would deny the unconditional nature of genuine personal commitment. And, within a Christian frame of reference, the model for marital love is itself unconditional. Lifelong intention, however, does not preclude the possibility of the violation and breaking of the covenant. Realism demands recognition of that potentiality, just as it did for the early Israelites with their covenant. This realism is the corollary of the idealism which demands that the intention of the covenant be lifelong and unconditional.

There is in addition something inherently future-oriented about sexual intercourse when it is authentic and person-centered. It is difficult in a real human relationship to say to one's sexual partner: "This is for tonight and tonight's kicks only. It has no implications for our future relationship." Even where the future of the relationship is cloudy, a future is already implied when two people go to bed together. And there is usually at least some illusion or hope that the relationship will have no *terminus ad quem,* that it is lifelong, forever. Witness the kind of eternity-oriented endearments which lovers whisper to one another in the act of lovemaking, whether or not they are married and whether or not the endearments reflect actual intentions.

What are the moral implications of this "foreverness" dimension of marriage? It implies that the sexual act is only proper in a relationship which has some promise of permanence, some innuendos of the eternal. This is not because it is immoral to have more than one sexual partner. It is rather because the sense that "I am for this person not only today but forever" is a symptom of the kind of relationship in which sexuality is realized more than exploited. Therefore, those who are married may need to acknowledge this lifelong intention every time they make love. And those who are unmarried may need to ask themselves why they are unwilling to acknowledge their lifelong intentions, or, if they are willing, why they are unwilling to publicize that acknowledgement. And those who are not persuaded that there is such a dimension to the sexual act may need to ask themselves whether sex is being realized or exploited in their relationship.

Let no one misconstrue these questions and challenges as an argument for limiting "moral" intercourse to married persons. They simply reflect the ideal with which a lifelong view of the marriage covenant confronts everyone who engages in intercourse, whether he is married or not.

Ronald S., a graduate student, and Cheryl P., an undergraduate, have known each other for six months and have been sleeping together for four when Cheryl announces that she is pregnant. They seek out a clergyman to ask if he will marry them immediately. Some brief exploration with each of them alone reveals that Ronald is not happy about the marriage, has consented only out of a vague sense of honor and some fear of scandal, and doubts very much that the union will last. He anticipates a divorce "within a few years," although he claims he is willing to give the relationship a chance. Cheryl is quite anxious to marry Ronald, although she recognizes his reluctance and that it does not bode well for their future together. She confesses that the pregnancy was precipitated by her through intentional carelessness in her birth control procedures. And she says that this was because every time they slept together Ronald reminded her that he didn't "want to get involved." He in turn affirms that he considered this the only "moral thing" to do, since it was simply honest.

What has happened here? Two young people have established a sexual relationship with an explicit denial of the dimension of lifelong intention. One has apparently been more honest in this than the other. And yet, each is now caught in a situation where the only "moral" solution seems to them to be to perpetuate the relationship without this dimension.

Is this the most responsible solution for all concerned? Is it, for example, the most promising solution for their child, given the present state of their relationship? And what should the clergyman have done? Where do his responsibilties in such a decision lie? To the church? To the couple? To some higher value, as he reads the foreseeable consequences of his decision?

SEX WITHIN THE COVENANT

It should be clear that from a new morality perspective the canons of sexual morality are the same for the married as for the unmarried. This is one of the earmarks of a new morality approach to sexual ethics, and serves to distinguish it from the prevailing old morality view. The old morality has already established marriage as a universal condition for "moral" sexual intercourse. This leads some to assume that there is one sexual morality for those who are married and another for those who are not. According to such thinking, sexual morality for the married has two basic tenets: (1) don't sleep with anyone but your marriage partner; and (2) don't engage in anything but "natural" heterosexual acts (where "natural" usually means conventional genital contact in a prone position).

The new morality challenges an arbitrary distinction between married and unmarried because it reflects a subtle but powerful moral double standard. For the new moralist, self-giving love is *the* moral criterion in all decisions, regardless of the formal context in which they are made. The new morality also challenges the old morality on the two laws which are generally prescribed for sex within marriage. *In context* both adultery and unconventional forms of sexual expression may be appropriate and moral.

ADULTERY

The question of adultery is a thorny one because it is one heterosexual practice which is explicitly forbidden in Scripture. Most new moralists will acknowledge that it is hard to imagine a specific situation in which infidelity would appear to be the most loving option. The scriptural proscription is, of course, consistent with a covenant understanding of marriage. It is also probably generally protective of the stability of the social order. In this, the seventh commandment reflects the same social concern as the rest of the decalogue. In most cases, having already bound oneself to a particular sexual partner, sex with another seems exploitative of someone. Given the institution of marriage and the vows which it reflects, part of the context of infidelity has already been determined. Whatever else it represents, and whatever moral values it may invoke, adultery involves the breaking of a vow. It always betokens some loss of faith. Consequently, it is properly called infidelity, even where the failure to keep faith is justified by appeal to a higher value than the marriage vows. In the bibli-

cal view, with its emphasis on keeping faith, it is natural that this act ·
should be viewed as disobedient and a violation of the God-man
covenant.

The strong taboos on adultery in Scripture are indices of how seriously the biblical writers felt on this subject. This contrasts with the
apparent lack of concern with which they viewed premarital intercourse, which is the object of stronger taboos than adultery in our
time. The Bible reveals no explicit concern with what is now properly
known as premarital intercourse. It reveals only that the biblical
writers were alarmed by adultery and its social implications. What is
more important, they understood the misuse of the body in sexual
acts to be essentially immoral. We should keep in mind that in those
passages which prohibit "fornication," the original language pro-
scribed simply the misuse of the body. This is reflected in Jesus's
reinterpretation of the Mosaic Law on this point in the Sermon on
the Mount:

> You have heard that it was said, "You shall not commit
> adultery." But I say to you that every one who looks at a
> woman lustfully has already committed adultery with her
> in his heart.[10]

That does not justify adultery. Nor is it an argument for the aboli-
tion of the seventh commandment. But neither is it an argument
which allows the demands of that commandment to be exhausted
by adherence to its letter. Like the rest of the Sermon on the Mount,
this is an appeal for fulfilling the law by internalizing its spirit. In
regard to adultery an illustration of the violation of that spirit is looking lustfully at a woman. What else does it mean to look lustfully at
a woman than to view her simply as a body/object rather than a
person/subject? That is the real burden of the seventh commandment. Don't use a person as an object! Don't misuse the body! And
insofar as adultery represents the breaking of the marriage contract,
it is assumed that it usually represents the misuse of the body of
another.

The general appropriateness of taboos on adultery notwithstanding, its prohibition should not become a moral absolute. In the same way, prohibitions against stealing and killing should not become moral absolutes in and of themselves. From a negative point of view, there are always situations which will be exceptions to the general rule. And from a positive point of view, keeping the spirit of that commandment is more important than its letter. Let the self-righteous married man who regularly commits adultery "in his heart" beware. The new morality calls his behavior as seriously into question as that of any more overt adulterer. But let the overt adulterer also beware. Let him ask himself what his infidelity says about his marriage vows and the present state of his marriage relationship. Let him ask himself to what extent the adulterous relationship involves the exploitation of the sexuality of another.

This then is the first implication of new morality thinking for sex within the covenant. It should not violate the covenant. And if it does, its only conceivable justification is through appeal to a higher covenant, that covenant which marriage at its best is intended to reflect.

UNCONVENTIONAL FORMS

The new morality also challenges the limitation of the forms of sex within marriage. Biblical passages concerning "unnatural" practices notwithstanding, any form of sexual expression is potentially moral insofar as it is appropriate to the meaning and depth of a relationship as perceived by the participants. This seems shocking to some, but should be self-evident to the reader who has grasped the moral rationale of new morality thinking. If the ultimate court of moral appeal is no formal code but rather a spirit of person-centered concern for the other, it follows that no form of sexual behavior is in and of itself immoral. Its relative morality or immorality will always depend on the relationship in which it is indulged. The prime contextual criteria will be the meaning and appropriateness of a particular act to the actors. This is its "naturalness" *for them* rather than its "naturalness" as determined by culturally relative criteria. For example, oral-genital contact is a form of sexual expression common to many marriages but socially and often legally tabooed. Some would hold that this practice is unnatural, perverted, and a distortion of human sexuality. According to new morality thinking, there are many relationships (including many marriages) in which this form of play might be utterly inappropriate and *therefore* immoral and exploitative. But there are also relationships (and not just among the married) in which it might be appropriate and a deeply satisfying realization of sexuality for both partners. Because this form of sexual expression seems especially intimate in the context of oral and genital attitudes which characterize our culture, it is probably more appropriate to relationships of considerable depth and duration. However, even this general observation cannot be made into a law.

Sex within the covenant then is subject to the same moral canon as sex outside the covenant. It is ultimately subject to this canon only, not to any more socially and historically relative expressions of it. Indeed, married people are even more bound by the ideal implied in a covenant view of marriage than are the unmarried (even though our society tends to preach responsibility more to the unmarried). This is because married people have explicitly affirmed this ideal.

SEX OUTSIDE THE COVENANT

The big moral questions that concern our time still have to do with sex outside marriage. That this is so indicates the extent to which our age is confused regarding sexual morality. It is also an indicator of other phenomena already cited, such as the double standard and the cult of the virgin.

Where neither partner is married and where both are viewed as eventually eligible for marriage is the focus of most of the current excitement about a sexual revolution. It is also in this realm that the new morality has gained some of its most dubious notoriety. Indeed, among the less well-informed, the new morality is often viewed as little more than a permissive argument for premarital intercourse.

The word *premarital* is a misnomer for the practices to which it is usually applied. The popular understanding of premarital intercourse is heterosexual union between two people who are not married, who have never been married, and who are usually young. For example, the phrase is rarely applied to intercourse between unmarried persons in their mid-forties. The phrase actually denotes intercourse between two parties who are not married, but intend to be married to each other. That is, their intercourse is literally premarital, before their marriage. A good deal of what is popularly called premarital intercourse actually falls into this class. Many young people still seem to feel a need to justify their sexual behavior according to the "sex for the married only" rationale. In some cultures (for example, in the Scandinavian countries), such genuinely premarital intercourse receives widespread social approval. It is not uncommon for engaged couples to honeymoon together before finalizing their covenant in formal vows. In such contexts, the question of the extent to which the covenant is finalized by the sexual act itself is usually left begging. Some would like to see a liberalizing of present-day American sexual standards and attitudes in this direction, while still restricting moral sex to a particular formal state. However helpful such a liberalizing might be in our present sexual malaise, the new morality will finally have no part of this. Such casuistry, however liberal, is still old morality. It still sets up formal definitions of right and wrong behavior. It still tries to define contexts and situations in advance, rather than leaving that determination to the individual. And it is finally questionable if the intention to marry makes intercourse any more appropriate to a relationship than marriage itself. There are specific contexts, occasions, and situations within marriage and engagement, just as outside marriage and engagement, which make generalized norms irrelevant and inapplicable. From a new morality perspective, the technically premarital state does not argue a special moral case either for or against intercourse. With appropriate caveats, *premarital* can then be used in a more popular sense to refer to what has here been called sex outside the covenant.

What kind of guidelines then does the new morality offer for sex outside the covenant? Of course, no new moralist is going to prescribe universal guidelines which might be translated into a new, more liberal law. All the new moralist can do is to raise certain questions which the participants must answer for themselves as honestly as they can. These questions reflect some of the contextual elements which one imagines in most premarital situations. Some of them have already been touched upon. For example, the meaning of the sexual act to the two parties is of central importance in reaching a judgment concerning its relative morality. Where, for two people, intercourse means serious commitment, the morality differs from a situation in which sex is casual for one partner, committed for the other. Likewise, the relative degree of mutual consent and the projected future of the relationship can be significant variables in the extent to which sexuality is exploited or realized. The person who consents out of fear of loss of popularity or out of sheer curiosity is operating in a different moral framework from one who consents out of a genuine desire for the self-giving fulfillment of a relationship.

THREE GENERAL QUESTIONS

Beyond these considerations, three basic questions of responsibility can usually be asked in the context of contemporary American life. Each of these questions reflects the social dimension of the sexual act. They concern respectively the assumption of social responsibility, procreative responsibility, and financial responsibility.

Social responsibility here refers to those other than one's sexual partner who will be directly or indirectly affected by one's sexual behavior. Most obviously, this responsibility focuses on parents and other family members who may have to bear the social stigma ascribed to sex outside the marriage covenant. The sexual hypocrisy of our society is therefore an important element in the context in which most decisions regarding premarital intercourse are made. This does not mean that decisions need to defer to that hypocrisy or the threat which it wields. But it does mean that those who engage in sex outside the covenant, risking the stigmata of society, are responsible for these foreseeable consequences of their behavior. Insofar as those consequences extend beyond themselves and touch upon the lives of others, premarital intercourse involves social responsibilities. This is true even where those most directly affected by the behavior openly condone it. The consequences are nonetheless the same. One of the questions for those who engage in sex outside the covenant then concerns their social responsibilities in terms of the implications of their behavior for others.

Also, our behavior, however conforming or deviant, helps to shape the future attitudes, practices, and mores of our society. No man can escape responsibility for the future attitudes and values of his own social order. And nowhere is this more clear than in the realm of sexual behavior, where changing patterns lead to an altered view of sexual morality for the next generation. To recognize this is not to argue against change. Indeed, in many cases, it may be to argue for it. It is simply to recognize that when one challenges prevailing mores one assumes the responsibility for their potential alteration. For example, insofar as what is written in these pages may alter the sexual attitudes and practices of some, the author must assume some responsibility for that change. At least he must assume it if he takes people seriously, if his ethics are person-centered. Likewise, each generation has the social responsibility not only to challenge the sexual attitudes and mores delivered to it, but also to refine them and shape the attitudes of its children. Does my behavior itself contribute to attitudes which will encourage the exploitation or the realization of sexuality in those who follow? That is a question which all must ask about their sexual behavior, but especially those who challenge the prevailing mores. It is a question which only the individual can answer in his context.

A second question concerns the procreative responsibilities of the sexual act. The widespread availability and effectiveness of modern birth-control devices notwithstanding, intercourse involves the potential creation of a human life. Responsibility for the act of creation and for the life which is created rests on the creators. One of the questions which the new morality asks, within or outside marriage, is whether this eventuality is taken seriously. Are the participants emotionally and economically prepared to assume the responsibilities of bringing a new life into the world? More important, what is their present attitude toward this person in his potentiality? Do they value his subjectivity? Is he a person, like themselves, to be granted his own moral freedom and to be related to and welcomed in his personal uniqueness? Or is he essentially a thing, an unfortunate inconvenience? Is he in his potential personhood simply some*thing* distasteful which will happen if one is not careful enough in his birth-control procedures? When the latter is the case (and it is frequently the case within marriage as well as outside marriage), then a person-centered ethic raises serious questions about the morality of the act which might create this person.

This is not simply a reiteration of the traditional argument: Don't do it because you might get pregnant! The availability of increasingly effective means of conception control makes such an argument today unpersuasive. Moreover, it is not a moral but a purely pragmatic argument (although moral considerations can be pragmatic when they take foreseeable consequences seriously). But this particular argument invokes no moral ideal beyond the fear of getting caught. In the confusion of many young people today, society is probably paying the price for its earlier moral shallowness in brandishing the threat of pregnancy as *the* deterrent to premarital intercourse. An authentic morality requires an ultimate value which is more universal in its applicability, less conditioned, less apt to be swept away by the advances of science and technology. The issue here is that, with or without the threat of social stigma and the inconvenience of an unmarried pregnancy, the heterosexual act has a procreative dimension. And one's attitude toward the potential child has moral significance. Is *his* personhood, even in its potentiality, being exploited?

Closely related is the moral question of financial responsibility. In our capitalistic society when two people get married they assume some economic responsibility for each other and for potential offspring. Sex outside the marriage covenant cannot abdicate this responsibility simply because it has not been legalized in a formal contract. If the law is not absolute in what it prohibits, it is also not exhaustive in what it requires. Some of those requirements are morally binding whether or not one has formally put himself under the law. In premarital intercourse, the legal prescriptions of economic responsibility are not technically binding. But in a person-centered morality, the responsibility is nonetheless there. Our laws in this regard generally reflect the double standard. They discriminate against the male by depersonalizing the female and making her inferior and dependent on him. But, morally, each is still responsible to the other. And this responsibility has implications for the distribution and use of private property.

Those who engage in sex outside of marriage, like those who marry, should therefore ask themselves if the implied sharing of property is included in their self-giving. Are they willing to assume financial responsibility for each other? Are they ready and willing to exercise financial responsibility toward their offspring? Such considerations, of course, could be construed as a virtual sexual disenfranchisement of the poor. But that is not the case. The financial responsibility of the sexual act is relative to the economic context and style of one's life. What might be financial responsibility and solvency for one man might be inappropriate and inadequate for another. For a rich man's son to take a mistress or bring a child into the world could be more immoral and irresponsible than the sexual behavior of an unwed pauper in a more authentic relationship.

In sex outside the covenant, financial responsibility then means recognizing money as an important medium of interpersonal responsibility in the cultural milieu in which we live. To ignore this is potentially to exploit those persons for whose material welfare one may stand responsible.

Sex outside the covenant also includes the possibility of forced marriages or so-called shotgun weddings. These represent in most cases a capitulation to prevailing sexual mores by those who have flaunted them. Such unions are often justified by participants or anxious parents as representing the proper assumption of the procreative and financial responsibilities cited above. Of course, some (technically) premarital intercourse eventuates in a hastened wedding day, due to pregnancy. This is not really therefore a *forced* marriage. However, most marriages made explicitly under the duress of pregnancy are probably bad risks and inadvisable. A covenant made under duress is really no covenant at all, since consent can rarely be said to be freely given.[11] Moreover, to force a marriage can be threatening to the institution of marriage itself. And it is certainly depersonalizing of the two individuals involved, to say nothing of the extent to which the child involved is dehumanized and made into a thing. What is most debilitating to the self-image of a child who knows he was conceived out of wedlock is not, as popularly assumed, the "shame" of his parents' act. This can be overcome if one is raised to take any kind of a critical attitude toward the hypocrisy of many social mores. What is not so easy to eradicate in such cases is the guilt the child can feel for being the occasion and cause of an unwilling alliance. Parents who counsel such marriages and young people who see them as the easiest way out of a sticky situation should ask themselves some serious questions about their motives. More serious consideration needs to be given to the foreseeable consequences of such a union, and the depersonalizing implications for all involved.

SEX AND MARRIAGE: A REAPPRAISAL

It remains to conclude this discussion of sex and marriage with a reappraisal of their interrelationship. If it is true that the same sexual morality holds for the unmarried as for the married; if it is true that the tying of intercourse to marriage encourages moral hypocrisy and creates unnecessary dilemmas; then perhaps we need to recast our sexual morality so that it is easier to have premarital relations and harder to get married.

To make intercourse outside the covenant of marriage easier certainly does not mean to remove the moral challenge which is involved. Indeed, it may mean to sharpen that challenge by focusing on the extent to which sexuality is realized or exploited rather than whether or not two people have gone through certain formalities. Making sex outside the covenant easier means a change in attitude toward premarital intercourse in the direction of greater social acceptability. Such a change would imply a society open to the possibility of genuine and responsible heterosexual relationships outside of the marriage bond. It would mean that many people would be relieved of the burden of concealing such relationships from public opinion. It might even lead to a more wholesome attitude toward sexuality itself, with correspondingly less emotional trauma associated with the heterosexual act. And the popular belief that greater social acceptance of sex outside the covenant would lead to sexual license and to disregard of all moral considerations is not demonstrable. From counseling and listening to college students involved in premarital affairs, I see no more evidence of sexual irresponsibility and license than I do among my married peers. Indeed, if anything, I see less.

With a liberalizing of attitudes toward premarital sex should go a tightening up of the relative ease with which people can get married, particularly within the church. If the covenant image is applicable, then the making of covenants should be taken more seriously, and the process itself should be made more difficult and demanding. This might mean a society in which progressively fewer people would get married with the church's blessing. And those who married would be made more aware of the seriousness and moral depth of a covenant understanding of marriage. In effect, marriage would be redeemed from its present relative triviality, and the soaring divorce rate might be significantly reduced. That could avoid a good deal of human tragedy which present confusion tends to aggravate. It might also encourage a fuller realization of human sexuality, both within and outside marriage.

There are probably very few who would oppose such changes in our contemporary patterns of life. But there are even fewer who will pay the twofold price of greater attention to those who are preparing for marriage and a change in the prevailing attitude toward sex outside marriage.

A recognition of this need has led me over the past several years to increase the amount of time spent with a couple in premarital counseling from three hours to eight or ten. Even this may not be enough. In the face of the casualness with which most people approach marriage, and the "use" of the church and its functionaries for this purpose, young couples need to be confronted with greater demands. And they may need to examine their relationship in greater depth before they are ready to make a genuine covenant. It is noteworthy that as the amount of my time spent in premarital counseling has increased, the nature of the topics covered in this counseling has deepened. This development is not unrelated to an increased counseling load with those engaged in sexual relations outside of marriage. The two go together: a greater acceptance of the potential authenticity of fully sexual unmarried relationships and a greater emphasis on the seriousness of the marriage vows.

5

beyond conventional

heterosexuality

W<small>E HAVE CAUTIONED</small> that morality has to do with more than sex. Another warning is now in order. It would be easy, particularly on the basis of the preceding chapter, to identify sexual morality exclusively with heterosexual behavior. Of course, this is not the case. Any form of sexual expression, whether it is generally considered natural or unnatural, raises questions of sexual morality. Any form of sexual behavior involves decision-making in regard to one's sexuality. This is true regardless of the ideological frame of reference in which particular behavior is justified. Therefore, it is as true of abstinence as it is of indulgence; it is as true of celibacy as it is of premarital intercourse. All are fit subjects of concern when our focus is sexual morality.

A college student who was a practicing homosexual once commented to me after a sermon on sex: "That's fine. But when are you clergy going to say something about sex other than premarital intercourse? When are you going to speak to us sexually disinherited?" His question is a good one. Particularly when moralizing on campus, the clergy also tend to limit sexual morality to heterosexual behavior. The phrase *sexually disinherited* is an apt reminder against this tendency.

The purpose of this chapter is to examine three forms of sexual self-expression other than the conventionally heterosexual. None of them is by definition immoral. Neither is any of them immune from the question, in a particular instance, of the extent to which sexuality is either realized or exploited. They are (1) abstinence, (2) masturbation, and (3) homosexuality. Each represents an area in which some hard rethinking of traditional mores is needed. And no discussion of the morality of sex is complete without these areas. Ironically, prevailing public opinion finds the first of these forms moral and the latter two immoral or unnatural.

ABSTINENCE

Abstinence is here understood as self-conscious refraining from overt sexual (usually genital) involvement and stimulation. In popular usage, abstinence generally refers to refraining from heterosexual intercourse, as in the case of unmarried virgins and celibate priests. But abstinence should be understood to include the decision to refrain from all overt forms of sexual expression and involvement. Here it shall include refraining from overt homosexual practices and from masturbation.

The word *abstinence* has been chosen intentionally to include temporary as well as permanent arrangements for sexual continence. Consequently, it includes the decision to wait for a while (for example, until one marries) as well as the decision to renounce sexual involvement for life, as with most celibacy.

The key point to be argued regarding abstinence is that it *is* a form of sexual expression. Assuming that we are all sexual creatures, the decision to abstain is as much an expression of the self as sexual being as any decision to indulge. Abstinence is as much a form of sexual behavior as any other form of sexual behavior. It can lead to either the realization or the exploitation of sexuality.

Abel Jeanniere, a French Roman Catholic priest, is very clear on this point. In discussing celibacy, he characterizes chastity as "one of the modes of living in search of optimum and specific human sexuality." And he continues:

> In this light, chastity would seem to be the renunciation
> of eroticism as the privileged expression of love, but not
> the renunciation of all modes of intimacy. The difficulty

then is to find a true expression of love in everyday activities. This difficulty is not theoretical but is inherent in the
life that takes the greatest risks. There are many ways of
expressing love, but they all commit us to losing ourselves
in order to find ourselves, without knowing whether or not
we shall. The task of the person vowed to chastity must be
to find a human way of expressing love in a more universal
but still concrete language.[1]

This discussion appears in a chapter which Jeanniere heads "The
Human Sexual Being and the Choices of Love." Abstinence here
becomes one of the choices of love, one way of expressing one's
sexual/loving nature. As such, it enters the decision-making realm
and situationally becomes a moral issue.

From a Protestant point of view and from a new morality perspective, the current ferment in the Roman Catholic Church regarding
celibacy is a healthy sign. It has radical implications for sexual
morality because it promises to remove sexual abstinence from a
long-standing position of moral privilege. In recognizing abstinence
as one way of expressing sexuality, we may begin to view tabooed
forms of sexual expression in the same light. It is noteworthy that
recent papal statements have stressed the practical advantages of
celibacy for the clergy without touching on its moral superiority.
While ostensibly holding the line for priestly celibacy, Pope Paul VI's
encyclical of June 1967 on this subject acknowledges that the nature
of the priesthood itself does not require celibacy. It simply asserts
that the church has found the unmarried state "highly suitable" for
the clergy.

This point of view is compatible with the moral perspective of the
present study. If sexual abstinence is simply preferable for the clergy
because of their particular context and role, moral universals are not
being invoked. Of course, this is still casuistry since the "case" of the
clergy is defined in general, all-inclusive terms rather than in specific
situational terms. A new moralist in the papal see would be more
likely to say that abstinence might be an appropriate expression of

sexuality and vocation for some clergy, an inappropriate expression for others. It all depends on specific situations.

The implication of this view for temporary abstinence, whether among the unmarried or the married, should be clear. There is nothing inherently moral about maintaining one's virginity until marriage. But neither is it inherently immoral, "chicken," or old-fashioned to do so, as some over-zealous campus libertines proclaim. Abstinence in this relationship may be appropriate, in another relationship inappropriate. It all depends on the situation, the extent to which the ends of person-centered responsibility are served, and how rigid or free one's decision for abstinence is. Likewise, abstinence this year might be responsible; next year irresponsible. One's situation and context change.

Some married people decide temporarily to refrain from sexual involvement, or to seek out forms of expression other than intercourse. Sometimes, this is for physical/medical reasons. Sometimes it is in response to the psychological and emotional state of the marriage relationship, and the extent to which sex can be loving in such a climate. This can be a very responsible decision. It can also become irresponsible if it is rigidified or if the parties do not feel free to re-evaluate their context.

These general illustrations lead to the moral question of whether sexuality is being realized or exploited in sexual abstinence. From a new morality perspective there is no universal answer to this question. It seems likely, for example, that in the vows of many celibates there is a genuine realization of human sexuality. Sex is sublimated in a particular vocation. It seems just as probable that for some celibates abstinence serves as an escape from the responsibilities of those concrete relationships which sex symbolizes. Under such circumstances, abstinence can exploit one's own sexuality. It can be misused, used as a thing. Father Jeanniere recognizes this pitfall:

> . . . priests and nuns, and even more the champions of various ideologies, deceive themselves with a thousand fabricated hardships of a difficult day-to-day existence.

> With our sacrifices for an ideal or for the future we cleverly conceal from ourselves our fear of throwing ourselves into the sea of a great passion in which man is metamorphosed. All this is not meant as an invitation to eroticism, but to take concrete relationships seriously.[2]

The same principle holds for more temporary forms of abstinence. Is the premarital virgin realizing or exploiting her sexuality? That depends on the situation and on her motives. Has the withholding of sex become a means of leading a hesitant boyfriend to the altar, for example? Is abstinence a way of avoiding meaningful and therefore demanding relationships with members of the opposite sex? Has it become a way of making one's decisions in advance, to avoid the uncertainties of a concrete situation? Or is abstinence simply appropriate to the relationships in which an individual is presently involved? Is it perhaps a choice based on a sober evaluation of foreseeable consequences?

These are difficult questions. They touch on the deeper levels of the psyche and call for an awareness of motivational factors which are not always conscious. But real decision-making always relies on conscious awareness, however limited. And such questions are the stuff of which moral responsibility is made. No new moralist will ever claim that moral responsibility is easy. But every new moralist will continue to raise these questions, for himself and for others. They make abstinence more clearly a choice which may be loving in some contexts, unloving in others. It may lead to the realization of sexuality in some contexts, to its exploitation in others.

Perhaps three brief cases will illustrate the variety of contextual options in regard to abstinence.

1. John S. determines, on entering college, that he will maintain his virginity until marriage. This decision is based partly on parental teaching, partly on religious heritage, partly on personal ideals and his anticipation of his marriage relationship. For three years he abstains, although subject to a number of opportunities in dating rela-

tionships and with prostitution in a foreign land. In each case he determines that intercourse would be either exploitative or inappropriate to a particular relationship. During his fourth year in college John meets the girl he wishes to marry. After some soul-searching they decide to sleep together until their graduation and marriage. The decision reflects the judgment of each of them that this is appropriate to their relationship, and should not be further postponed. Precautions against conception are taken. This is a case of both temporary abstinence and a situational decision to forsake that abstinence, to overrule an earlier decision. Was he morally responsible? Were his decisions free? Was sexuality being exploited? In his abstinence? In his decision not to abstain?

2. Peter D. is a Roman Catholic who is moved toward a vocation of social service, and determines to enter the priesthood. This seems to him the most appropriate vocation for his calling to a helping role with underprivileged people. But it also involves vows of celibacy and refraining from something which has been part of his life in the past. On the other hand, it appears to Peter that sexual abstinence may be an important prerequisite of his functioning as a priest in the inner city. He is white and middle class, and has genuine reservations about requiring a wife and children to share his lot in that environment. And he sees the options for non-exploitative sex outside marriage for a priest to be relatively minimal. Therefore, Peter takes the vows.

Was he morally responsible? Was he true to himself and his values? Was his decision a free one? Was he exploiting or realizing his sexuality?

3. Susan T. is a young college woman who finds herself in a deep relationship with the man she believes she loves. She has been raised in a liberal Jewish environment in which premarital intercourse is explicitly tabooed but tacitly condoned. She feels no real family or religious deterrents to sleeping with him, but experiences disturbing fears of pregnancy and the social stigma of an unmarried pregnancy.

She has no doubt that full sexual involvement would be appropriate to the relationship in question. Susan and her fiancé regularly engage in petting to orgasm and some oral-genital lovemaking. But she finally reaches the decision to abstain from intercourse until they are married.

Was she morally responsible? Was she free? Was she realizing or exploiting her sexuality? Her fiancé's sexuality?

MASTURBATION

What Richard Hettlinger calls "sex alone"[3] is common in our culture, particularly among the unmarried. In spite of taboos against it and myths concerning its aftereffects, masturbation perseveres as one of the simplest and most popular ways of achieving sexual satisfaction and release.

The word *masturbation* can cover a variety of practices from self-induced genital orgasm to simple fondling of self and other more subtle forms of autoerotic play. But the word here is used in its popular meaning of sexual self-stimulation—primarily genital, usually to orgasm, and most often manual. As such, masturbation is probably more common among men than among women, although it appears to be commonplace with both sexes.

Of course, the relative commonness of masturbation is not relevant to moral considerations, except when its assumed unnaturalness is pleaded as a moral case against it. Those who would condemn masturbation outright on "natural" moral grounds must therefore come to grips with indications that this practice is at least normative, if not also natural.

There is probably no other sexual practice which is subject to such ambivalent public sentiments and such a wide variety of private convictions. In our psychologically sophisticated but morally naïve time, masturbation is officially both frowned on and winked at at the same time. Most people seem to view it as a reprehensible practice, at best a stage in psychosexual development, but clearly unnatural or even perverted. But the same people often tend to dismiss reports of masturbation with the reminder that "boys will be boys." On the other hand, there are those among the sexual *avant-garde* who consider masturbation such a universal phenomenon that to reach sexual maturity without engaging in it is considered abnormal or inhibited. Certainly psychiatrists in our time, who tend to set norms for social behavior, seem to be of the overwhelming opinion that masturbation (except where compulsive) is no cause for alarm.

This public ambivalence has led to moral and emotional confusion among young people who masturbate. Among college students, for example, it is probable that the majority feel some residual guilt over this practice but justify it to themselves intellectually. There are, of course, continuing religious taboos against masturbation, particularly within Roman Catholicism where it is seen as a repetition of the biblical sin of Onan.[4] But religious taboos appear to carry less and less weight with the well-educated younger generation, who seek rationales, not taboos. Hence we may be headed for a crisis in our moral view of masturbation when changes in ideology catch up with the changes in practice which are already effective.

It should also be noted that masturbation is not limited to the unmarried or others without regular sexual partners. There is reason to believe that it is more common among married people than is generally assumed, and that it is quite common in those who engage in heterosexual relations outside marriage and among practicing homosexuals. All of these types of relationships represent contextual factors which are relevant to any moral discussion of masturbation.

What then is the morality of masturbation? Is it moral or immoral? Can one say anything about it inherently?

Certainly masturbation, like homosexuality, abstinence, and conventional intercourse, is a form of sexual expression. It is a way of saying who one is sexually. It represents a choice. It is one of a series of alternatives for sexual self-expression. Masturbation is then neither inherently moral nor inherently immoral. Its morality depends on its context, its meaning in context, and the motives with which it is practiced.

The whole moral issue hangs, as with other sexual practices, on the extent to which sexuality is realized or exploited. It depends on the extent to which masturbation situationally is a loving or an unloving act. Some will have difficulty imagining how sex alone can be loving or unloving. But that is just the point. Because masturbation is ordinarily carried on in solitude does not mean that it is isolated from the world of interpersonal relationships. People who masturbate are involved in a myriad of relationships, and their masturbation can both reflect and affect these relationships. But it can also represent an escape from the threat and the responsibility of authentic heterosexual involvement.

From a new morality perspective, therefore, those who masturbate need to ask themselves some hard contextual questions regarding the role of "sex alone" in their lives. Is it an escape, a kind of semi-sex because the prospect of other alternatives is too discomforting? Or, can masturbation be a choice for sexual fulfillment when other alternatives seem pragmatically or morally inappropriate? What are the alternatives? Abstinence? Intercourse? Homosexuality? For many young men in our society, intercourse is not a live option for prolonged periods of time because of military service or imprisonment. Does this contextual factor alter the morality of masturbation for them? Ironically, in the U.S. Navy, masturbation is still grounds for discharge, although anyone who has served knows of its prevalence on board ship.

Where masturbation is practiced within the context of a regular sexual relationship, the individual may need to ask himself what effect his masturbation has on the relationship. In marriage, for example, masturbation can be an act of disloyalty akin to adultery, surrogate sex which avoids sexual confrontation with one's partner. But in marriage, masturbation can also represent a sensitive, person-centered choice for sexual fulfillment in the face of contextual factors (e.g., physical or emotional disorder) which make intercourse seem exploitative or manipulative. Some married people prefer masturbation to what appears to them, at least temporarily, to be "using" their partners. Is this necessarily an immoral choice? Are our taboos on masturbation so strong that the only moral alternative open to individuals in such situations is abstinence?

And what about adolescents and young adults who masturbate in preference to or out of lack of opportunities for premarital intercourse? What of the young man who has determined that the risks and involvements of premarital coitus are more than he can responsibly assume? Is abstinence the only moral alternative for his sexual expression at a time when his sexual potency is probably at its peak? And what are we teaching him about his sexuality when we tell him that abstinence is the only moral alternative before marriage? Can such allegedly moral teaching itself exploit sexuality?

Perhaps the following real situations will point up the variety of contextual factors involved in passing moral judgments on masturbation.

1. Carol F. marries after a full heterosexual relationship with her husband before marriage. Before marriage she had also masturbated more or less regularly, and always to orgasm. When she began sleeping with her fiancé she stopped masturbating. She always achieved orgasm in premarital coitus. But after marriage she finds that she is frequently left unfulfilled by intercourse. She considers returning to masturbation without her husband's knowledge. But she experiences guilt feelings at this prospect, feels that it would be disloyal to him, and fears that it would be potentially disruptive of their relationship. So she determines to bring herself manually to orgasm after coitus, with her husband's full knowledge. She even asks him to hold her during masturbation, attesting to the basically interpersonal nature of the practice in her eyes.

Granting the many complicated factors in this relationship, and that the husband's sexual responsibility might be called into question, was her masturbation a responsible act? Was it person-centered? Was she realizing or exploiting her sexuality?

2. Lenny M. is a young graduate student who masturbates regularly, virtually daily. He is extremely shy and retiring in social contacts. He has had no sexual experience at age twenty-four beyond a few kisses with a girl at a college party. This incident was very arous-

ing and frightening to him. He feels mildly guilty over his masturbation, but does not see it as a problem and has come to accept it as his "lot." He comes seeking counseling help over his anxiety in the presence of young women and his apparent inability to relate to them in any meaningful way. As he sees it, his masturbation is not related to this problem. He feels, however, that if he should make a successful marriage he would probably cease masturbating. He has tried to give up masturbation on several occasions without success, and has now determined that it is inevitable.

Granting the uncertainty of cause and effect in such a situation, was his acceptance of his own masturbation responsible? Was his decision to continue free? What foreseeable consequences does his decision have for his relationships with others? What foreseeable consequences does it have for his basic problem with women?

3. Ronald G. is an elderly Protestant clergyman who has masturbated all his life. In the same period he has married and raised a family of five children. His masturbation has always been private, and to his knowledge not even his wife has been aware of it. His marriage has ostensibly been a happy and successful one, although he acknowledges that his married sex life has been "routine and unexciting." He masturbated before marriage, and at the time of marrying determined to continue this practice because it was personally fulfilling and not apparently damaging to anyone. He has never felt strongly attracted sexually to his wife, although he has been attracted to other women. However, he considers adultery a violation of a vow and potentially destructive of a number of relationships. He feels some guilt over his masturbation vis-à-vis social mores and his role as a clergyman, but has justified it to himself within his own moral frame of reference.

Granting the subtle interplay of cause and effect between his lackluster marital sex life and his satisfying solitary sex life, does his masturbation seem morally responsible or irresponsible? What were his alternatives? To what extent was he realizing or exploiting his sexuality? His wife's?

4. Emily H. is a postmenopause spinster in her mid-forties. As a young woman she had some heterosexual experience, sleeping for a while with a young man she planned to marry. Shortly after his accidental death she determined on a vocation of social service in which she would have more freedom to be effective if she were single. Although she did not decide not to marry at this time, she did begin to curtail her dating life. She also began masturbating, at first experimentally, subsequently on a regular basis. She found this to be a self-satisfying form of sex life. She apparently feels no guilt over this practice and continues to masturbate. She now sees masturbation as a way of expressing herself sexually which is most compatible with her needs and vocational responsibilities.

Is her decision a moral one? Does it seem to be free? Is she escaping heterosexual responsibilities or simply expressing sexual responsibility in her own way? To what extent is she exploiting or realizing her sexuality?

HOMOSEXUALITY

Homosexuality has been touched upon in our discussion of attitudes toward maleness and femaleness and the double standard. It remains to examine the morality of homosexuality as a form of sexual expression, parallel to abstinence, masturbation, and intercourse.

Setting homosexuality in this context may surprise those who view it as socially debilitating and by definition immoral. For such thinking, which still dominates many of our statutes, the morality of homosexual practices is not an open question. Homosexuality is viewed as masturbation is still viewed in some quarters, as essentially unnatural, a crime against nature, and therefore immoral.

Of course, from a person-centered ethical perspective, the only crimes against nature are crimes against people.[5] These are acts which reduce persons to things or have dehumanizing consequences. Therefore, the new moralist begins by dismissing moral objections to homosexuality based on an assumed "natural" law. The problem with natural law thinking is that what is assumed to be natural is really arbitrary and relative to the social milieu of the person making the judgment. For example, it is often assumed that the anatomical structure of male and female genitalia determines the natural function of sexuality. But, without ignoring the important reproductive function of sexuality, one can recognize that sex serves a number of other functions in human life. The judgment that sex is only for reproduction is as limited to an agrarian, low-population economy as the judgment that pearls are valuable is to a consumer economy. In the realm of sexual morality, the only thing that is "natural" is that human beings have sexual needs and desires. And even then, it can be "natural" to sublimate those needs and desires for vocational or ideological reasons, as in some self-conscious abstinence. No sexual arrangement, no particular form of sexual expression can be cited as *the* natural one. All are subject to the same moral criterion.

Before examining the morality of homosexual acts, a definition is needed. The word *homosexual* can be used to refer to various subtle gradations of erotic attraction or involvement between members of the same sex. As such, it can cover everything from latent expression in affection between school chums to overt expression in genital contact. Here the term will be limited to overt sexual (usually genital) relations between members of the same sex.[6] Such a definition does not ignore the psychological significance of more subtle expressions of homosexual tendencies. It does, however, seek to limit our moral considerations to self-conscious choices in the realm of overt behavior. It focuses our discussion on homosexuality as a chosen form of sexual expression.

One moral consideration which distinguishes homosexual practices from abstinence and masturbation is legality. Unlike abstinence, unlike masturbation in most instances, and unlike premarital intercourse in many instances, homosexuality is subject to legal penalties in most states of the union. In spite of recent attempts[7] to alter the law, the context in which one decides to engage in a homosexual act is still usually colored by the fact that this is a decision to operate outside the law. From a new morality perspective, this does not make the act immoral, since person-centered ethics are always open to breaking the civil law in the name of their own ideal. But illegality is still a contextual factor, just as it is for one who engages in civil disobedience, regardless of the justness of his cause. Contextually, the present legal sanctions against homosexuality mean that the homosexual subjects himself and his partner to legal reprisals, possible blackmail, and a generally secretive existence. All of that may be worth the goal. But these risks represent foreseeable consequences which must be taken seriously in reaching an individual moral judgment.

Against this background, what are we to say? To what extent is sexuality realized or exploited by the homosexual? Under what conditions is it conceivable that this form of socially deviant sexual behavior might represent a morally responsible choice? Under what conditions does it seem irresponsible, socially debilitating, exploitative of sexuality or other individuals?

Suspending the question whether some individuals are physiologically and biochemically predisposed to homosexual activity, it seems clear that many individuals are psychologically oriented in this direction, and find fulfillment in homosexual relationships. Given such a population, is it society's role to moralize and legalize about their behavior? This question holds whether the moralizing uses overt terms like *sin* or subtle terms like *sickness*. The moral/legal question should still be: In what way is the homosexual's chosen form of sexual expression harmful to other individuals, to himself, or to society as a whole? It is on the basis of this kind of question that many recent investigators have appealed for a change in the law. Their case is that while homosexuality can be exploitative where it involves coercion, the seduction of an "innocent" minor, or the creation of a public nuisance, it is not a legal problem when the act takes place between consenting adults in private.

From a new morality perspective it is possible to say that homosexuality may not even be a *moral* problem in some cases between consenting adults in private. Person-centered ethics hold firmly to the potentiality of two people of the same sex to find sexual fulfillment in one another and to realize their sexuality in their relationship. This is a rejection of the heterosexual mystique, the assumption that heterosexual relationships have some ontological or natural authority which cannot be extended to other relationships. Where the realization of sexuality means the realization of personhood through sex, there seems no reason to exclude homosexual relationships from this possibility. The moral question for the homosexual, as for the heterosexual, becomes the extent to which sexuality is realized or exploited in the relationship.

The practicing homosexual must therefore ask himself some of the same questions which parties to heterosexual relationships (married or unmarried) need to ask: To what extent does this act have the same meaning and implications for both of us? To what extent is either of us using the other as a thing, an instrument for the fulfillment of his own particular needs? To what extent is our decision to engage ourselves homosexually reached freely? To what extent am I being true to myself in this act? In this relationship?

Likewise, the practicing homosexual may need to ask some of the same questions suggested for the sexual abstainer and the masturbator. Is this an escape from the responsibilities of heterosexual involvement? Or is it the most appropriate means to a full sexual expression of who I am? What are the alternatives to this particular form of sexual behavior? Given all of the contextual factors (including, for most, illegality), is this truly fulfilling for me? Am I happy with this form of sexual expression?

Perhaps the following real-life cases will indicate the number of complicated contextual factors at play in any decision to engage in homosexual activity.

1. Michael P. is a college senior who has been engaged in homosexual relationships since his freshman year. His first experience came when he was "picked up" by an older man in a large city. His own participation initially was with consent and largely out of curiosity. Michael is a handsome youth, self-assured and popular with girls. He confesses, however, that he feels some anxiety about establishing a lasting heterosexual relationship and that he does not find women attractive sexually. He has masturbated on and off both be-

fore and during his homosexual period. He is living with another young man in a homosexual relationship when he comes seeking counseling help. The main complaint is that he feels his homosexual behavior is no longer freely elected, where he once thought it was. He also feels that, although sexually satisfying, it leads to repeated dead ends in his relationships with homosexual partners and to personal suffering. He seeks counseling help to rid himself of what seems to him a debilitating and nonproductive "habit."

What is the morality of such a situation, in both his initial involvement and subsequent desire to withdraw? Where is he acting responsibly and where irresponsibly? Clearly, from Michael's point of view, his behavior has become irresponsible at the point where it has become unfree. It is also irresponsible in his eyes because it leads to consequences which are debilitating to himself and others. What is the morality of his relationship with his roommate? And how free or unfree is his decision to terminate it? What are the consequences of this behavior for other relationships? These are questions which only Michael can finally answer. But, from a new morality perspective, the relative responsibility of his behavior will hang largely on the answers.

2. Robert B. is an unmarried Protestant clergyman in his mid-forties. He has never been sexually involved with a woman, although he feels meaningfully related to a number of women, married and unmarried, within his congregation. Since his early thirties and a conscious decision not to marry, he has been a practicing homosexual in a series of carefully selected and discreet relationships with men of similar age, tastes, and educational background. His decision not to marry seems to have been based more on an increasing preference for living alone than on homosexual appetites or vocational considerations. Indeed, professionally it is probably to his disadvantage to be unmarried. He has never had a roommate and does not tend to establish exclusive or lasting homosexual relationships. However, he may engage in homosexual activity with the same partner off and on over several years. He has not ever knowingly introduced

anyone to homosexuality, and he tends to find his partners among experienced homosexuals who move in the same social circles Robert does. He professes no guilt about his behavior, although he deems it important for himself and others to be extremely discreet about it.

What is the morality of Robert's behavior? In what ways is it responsible or irresponsible? Whom does his behavior affect? What are its foreseeable consequences? What indications are there that sexuality is realized or exploited? How free do his decisions appear to be?

3. Jean V. is a twenty-five-year-old schoolteacher who has been a practicing homosexual for four years. She has never been sexually involved with a man although she is physically attractive, and dates more or less regularly. She was introduced to homosexual activity by an older fellow teacher during her first year out of college. She has since introduced a number of other young women, usually professional colleagues, to homosexual practices. She sees this as a matter of free adult consent on their part and confesses no moral qualms about it. But she has strong moral inhibitions against making homosexual advances to any of her high school students. She tends to establish romantic attachments with her homosexual partners which can be quite intense for several months before ultimately breaking up. Although personally painful to her, she accepts this pattern as inevitable in the light of what she considers social hypocrisy concerning homosexuals. She intends to continue her homosexual patterns for life and not to marry. She believes that this is the most satisfying and appropriate form of sexual expression for her personally.

What are the implications of a person-centered morality for such a real-life situation? Is Jean exploiting her own sexuality or that of others? In regard to herself, she clearly does not think so. Who else can judge? What are the foreseeable consequences of her behavior, for herself and others? Does it seem socially responsible? What complicated moral considerations bear on her introducing other "innocent" parties to her homosexual patterns? What of the necessary secretiveness of her behavior? What implications does it have for her role as a teacher? One can only conjecture the real answers to these questions. But they should show how thoroughly gray and contextual, rather than black and white, the morality of homosexual practices is.

TWO RELATED ISSUES: ABORTION AND THE USE OF DRUGS

Our discussion would seem incomplete without a brief consideration of two related issues—abortion and the use of drugs in relation to sexual activity. Both represent serious moral issues. Neither is directly an act of sexual expression. But both are closely related to sexual acts. Both abortion and a drug-sex relationship are also relatively common in the present college generation, and represent areas of moral concern for many students. What then are the implications of a situational approach to decision-making on these two issues?

ABORTION

The morality of voluntarily terminating the life of an unborn child has long exercised theologians and moralists. The issue seems to have been focused anew in recent years by a combination of factors. These include a weakening of traditional taboos on intercourse outside of marriage, a new questioning of taboos on abortion itself, the social stigma and inconvenience of an unmarried pregnancy, increasingly safe and effective means of abortion, and the availability of medical practitioners for this service. Some of these factors are interrelated, and contribute to one another. All of them have conspired to create a climate in which abortion is a live option for large numbers of women, married as well as unmarried.

The possibility of abortion as a solution to an unwanted pregnancy cannot help but have its effect on the sexual behavior of these women. One of the contextual factors in their decision-making regarding sex is, in effect, in the process of change. This means that more and more young women may be expected to be confronted with a concrete decision about whether or not to have an abortion. It is to their situation that the present discussion is addressed. The morality of the social context which makes abortion a live option or a moral crisis is an important question, but one beyond the scope of the present study. Our concern here is with concrete decision-making about abortion as an issue related to sexual behavior.

There seem to be three prevailing moral positions regarding abortion in contemporary American culture. The first is that it is immoral because it involves taking a human life, which is tantamount to murder.[8] This has been the classic position of the Roman Catholic Church, and it is still backed up by the statutes of many of our states. According to such thinking, the morality of abortion is not a debatable question. Abortion is inherently immoral, regardless of circumstances, because it is contrary to divine and natural law.

A second position on abortion is that of the casuists and the neo-casuists. Their argument is that there are certain identifiable situations in which abortion is justified and advisable. Such circumstances might be pregnancy through incest or rape, the foreseeable death of the mother through delivery, or predictable hardship worked on a family through the addition of another child. Accidental and inconvenient pregnancies, whether married or unmarried, are rarely included by the casuists. The virtue of this position is that it moves beyond the legalism of absolute prohibition and provides a working argument for liberalizing legislation. After all, if the letter of the law is to be changed, it must be changed in a casuist way—by defining those cases which stand outside the general provisions of the law. But casuist concessions are virtually irrelevant to the majority of women who seek abortions. These women are not in what is socially defined as an *in extremis* situation, although the situation may personally seem very extreme to them. These are the unmarried high school, college girls, and young professional women, and no small number of married women for whom another child seems to promise undue emotional strain on marriage and family relationships.

To moralize with such people about their sexual behavior—to suggest that they should have been more cautious or should have abstained—is irrelevant to their present situation. Likewise, to propose that they should now pay the price for their carelessness or irresponsibility is to miss the point of their moral dilemma. It also proposes moral retribution at the cost of human fulfillment and welfare, something which is not consistent with the spirit of person-centered ethics. It can also be to use the law in a way that, in effect, discriminates against women.

A third alternative is a thoroughly contextual view of the morality of abortion. This asserts that there are all kinds of individual as well as general cases in which abortion may be morally right. It suggests that the final moral criterion is whether abortion seems the most loving, responsible solution to the present situation for all concerned. This involves a realistic appraisal of the foreseeable consequences of abortion and its alternatives. Those who moralize in this realm should not forget that the alternatives to abortion also need justifying. The decision not to have an abortion with an unwanted pregnancy, for example, is a decision to handle the pregnancy in another way. What are the foreseeable consequences of this alternative? What is the morality of this solution?

The woman who contemplates an abortion also has some serious questions to ask herself. One of them concerns the present illegality of abortion in most states. Just as with homosexuality, this is a real contextual factor which involves added risks for herself, the practitioner involved, perhaps her parents, family, and others. And motivation is also a key factor. She must consider these questions: What are my real reasons for not wanting this child? Are they consistent with the ideals I espouse in other decisions? What are the feelings of the child's father, whether married or unmarried? What implications will this decision have for future decision-making in regard to sexual behavior? What are the foreseeable consequences for my relationship with the child's father? What about the child's life in its potentiality? How do I view it, and is it mine to take in this situation? Am I being true to myself? Can I live with this decision more creatively than I could live with the child? What effect may an abortion have on others close to me? And what about the practitioner? Is he being coerced? Is he responsible? Am I being responsible with myself in putting myself in his hands?

Obviously, from a new morality perspective, there is nothing inherently immoral about abortion, and the decision to obtain an abortion is just as gray and contextual as all other decisions. Perhaps the following cases will point this up.

1. Judy L. is in her junior year in college when she discovers that she is pregnant. The father is her fiancé, whom she plans to marry in fifteen months; he is the only man she has ever slept with. Judy is a respected leader on her campus and a girl with a promising career in graduate school ahead of her. Still, the prospect of an abortion is distasteful to her, more for emotional reasons than on strictly moral grounds. Her fiancé is willing to defer to her feelings and marry now for the sake of the child. He would, however, prefer an abortion in the light of his own plans for graduate school. Judy's mother is strongly opposed to her delivering the child or marrying at this time, partly because of certain dreams for her daughter's education, partly because of the social stigma which friends and family would attach to the pregnancy. In the end, Judy defers to the strong preferences of her mother and the mild preferences of her fiancé and obtains an abortion.

How responsible or irresponsible was this decision? Was Judy being true to herself? To her ideals? How free was her decision? Was it person-centered? To what extent was she exploiting or realizing herself? What were the foreseeable consequences for the alternatives?

2. Marianne P. is in her senior year in college when she becomes pregnant by her fiancé, whom she plans to marry after graduation in June. She is a conspicuous leader on her campus. There is no possibility of concealing the pregnancy until June. Furthermore, Marianne comes from a very prominent and conservative old southern family. She knows her family would be deeply mortified and hurt by a premature marriage, an early baby, and failure to graduate. In addition, her fiancé is a student at a military academy where marriage in course means dismissal. In spite of a promising record and future in the military, he is willing to marry now if that is her choice. Most of the practical factors in the situation seem to argue

for an abortion and keeping the whole matter secret from Marianne's family. But she feels strong personal aversion to an abortion and questions its morality in her case. Consequently, she and her fiancé finally decide to go through with the pregnancy, marry, interrupt her education and tell all to her parents. They also decide to keep their marriage a secret from friends until after his graduation, to protect his status.

How responsible was their decision in regard to abortion? Was it made on person-centered grounds? What were the foreseeable consequences for this decision? What would they have been if Marianne had had an abortion? What were the implications of either decision for her future relationship with the child's father? For her relationship with her parents? What would her parents have preferred, had they been given the choice? Does the fact that the marriage involved temporary dishonesty alter the moral choice?

3. Frank M. is a young Protestant clergyman in his early thirties, apparently happily married with four small children. In a very rural parochial setting his salary is minimal with no great promise of increase in the foreseeable future. When his wife discovers that she is pregnant with their fifth child, both of them agree that this will put undue emotional and financial strain on the whole matrix of family relationships. Neither of them is averse to the idea of an abortion. Frank's wife actually desires it in preference to another child. But the families of both raise strong objections, and there is some vocational hazard to Frank involved. Still, after due consideration, they find a doctor whom they consider responsible and obtain an abortion.

Was this a responsible act? Was it free? What were the alternatives? What were the foreseeable consequences of the abortion and of the alternatives? What weight should family opinion and vocational considerations carry in a person-centered decision? Are questions of inherent morality or general cases at all relevant to the deliberations of Frank and his wife?

4. Early in her senior year in college, Barbara L. finds that she is pregnant. The child's father is the only man with whom she has had

sexual relations and the man she has planned to marry. Marriage is her preferred alternative in the face of the pregnancy. However, her lover is unwilling to marry at this time, apparently because it would involve terminating his education for financial reasons. His family is anxious to assume all costs of an abortion, and this is the alternative urged on Barbara by both him and her own family. Abortion, however, appears to Barbara to involve taking a life which it is not hers to take, however much justified by contextual considerations. The prospect of an abortion is also quite distasteful to her personally. Consequently, she determines to leave school, deliver the child in a reasonably anonymous setting, give it up for adoption, and resume her education. She accepts considerable financial assistance from the father's family to this end. Although this is very upsetting to her own family, she perseveres in her decision.

Is the morality of this decision independent of contextual factors? What makes it right or wrong? Has she taken the foreseeable consequences of her decision seriously? Has she dealt responsibly with all the persons involved, including her child? What about the decision to place the child for adoption? Can this be made now, before the fact? What are the implications of these decisions for her future relationship with the child's father or with other men? Will she live more comfortably with these decisions than with their alternatives?

SEX AND DRUGS

With the emergence of the so-called drug problem, a new dimension has been added to the morality of sex for some young people. Many of the drugs popular in our youth culture, particularly marijuana and LSD-25, have the dual effect of releasing inhibitions and heightening perceptions and sensitivity. It should come as no surprise, therefore, that some form of overt sexual experience has become an important part of the drug cult in our time.[9] This means that those who make a decision to experiment with drugs may at the same time be making a decision to experiment with sex. As with abortion, the use of drugs then becomes a moral issue related to sexual behavior.

The morality of the use of drugs—or any stimulant, depressant, or reality-changer—is beyond the scope of this discussion. Although some good clinical studies are available,[10] a sensitive and well-informed moral discussion of this increasingly common phenomenon has yet to appear. It is sufficient to note in passing that the same moral considerations should bear on the use of any agent which alters one's view of reality, or is a means of self-consciously suspending one's moral judgment. This means that parents who are quick to decry drug usage in the present student generation may need to take a hard look at the use of alcohol by their own generation.[11]

Our concern here, however, is with the use of drugs specifically in relation to sexual behavior. This means particularly the hallucinogens which can be used to remove psychological and moral barriers to sexual activity and to heighten the pleasure derived from sexual acts. For this reason, marijuana and LSD ("pot" and "acid" respectively) are peculiarly susceptible to being used for seduction, whether of oneself or of another.

The user of drugs for specifically sexual ends, therefore, needs to ask himself some serious questions about his needs and motives. For example, is this "trip" necessary? Do I need this particular kind of reality manipulator in order to realize my sexuality? If so, why? What does this say about me and my sexuality? Am I exploiting or realizing my sexuality in expressing it under these conditions? Am I exploiting or realizing the sexuality of another?

Again, if the drug is used simply to release inhibitions, what is the source of these inhibitions? Do they represent the real "me"? Is it realistic or exploitative to remove them in this way? What is the morality of self-consciously anesthetizing one's conscience? The answer to that may depend on how oppressive or realistic one's conscience is perceived to be. Sometimes what appears to be the voice of conscience is not oneself at all, but rather an "external locus of evaluation." Such voices may need silencing in the name of psychic health as well as morality. But is this a realistic way to do it?

If the drug is used to heighten one's sexual pleasure by heightening perceptions, a new series of moral questions emerges. Basically, it revolves around a philosophical question: What is real and what is unreal? What is real sex and what is unreal sex? It is possible that the use of external stimulants to intensify sexual release could be both therapeutic and fulfilling of one's sexuality. It could be real. It is also possible that it could be highly manipulative and exploitative of oneself or another. It could be unreal.

All of this indicates that the drug user should be aware of the sexual implications of usage. It also indicates that he is morally responsible for the decision to use the drug and for the sexual behavior which the drug evokes, whether intended or unintended. Perhaps the following actual situations will point up this responsibility.

1. Alice C. is a college senior who had her first intercourse when she was a freshman. It was in a casual relationship, and she now sees her own motivation as largely "out of curiosity." Since then she has slept with a number of men, although she is selective about her partners, and does not see herself as promiscuous. In her sophomore year she began using drugs, at first experimentally in social contexts, now more or less habitually. She started with diet pills—"dex," or dexedrine—then moved on to marijuana and LSD. She still uses all three in decreasing order of frequency, taking "dex" as a regular stimulant and using "pot" and "acid" in social contexts and "for kicks." She has discovered that sexual activity is more enjoyable for her when she is using marijuana or LSD, and now regularly takes one or the other in conjunction with sexual activity. She claims that by comparison sex without hallucinogens is dull, and she would never have it that way by choice. She also feels that this has not in any way made her more promiscuous. She plans to continue to use the hallucinogens for this purpose, although she intends to cut out the use of "dex" because she has been alarmed by its effect on her health.

What is the morality of this whole situation? Has the use of drugs changed Alice's sexual behavior? Her morals? To what extent have drugs become an agent for the exploitation or the realization of her sexuality? The sexuality of another? To what extent is the realization of her sexuality dependent on drugs? Is this necessarily exploitative?

Morally wrong? What is the difference between Alice's use of hallucinogens and the use of alcohol in relation to sex? Why is Alice using
drugs for sex? To anesthetize her conscience? To heighten her perceptions? Both?

2. Mary B. is a young married woman. She and her husband are
sexually faithful to one another, and see this as an important part of
their marriage vows. Each had a number of premarital affairs, and
they slept together for several months before marrying. There are no
children. Neither Mary nor her husband has ever used drugs, but
they move in social circles where the use of hallucinogens is common. Both are curious as to the effect of this on them and on their sex
life, which they consider adequate. By mutual consent they decide to
experiment with drugs together, and smoke "pot" at a party one
evening. They are self-consciously seeking a sexual effect. They
achieve the desired result in terms of released inhibitions, but not in
terms of heightened pleasure. The end result is exhibitionism in
front of their friends and subsequent embarrassment and disappoint-
ment. They resolve to carry on their sex life henceforth without the
help of drugs. In effect, they learned what they wanted to know from
the experiment, although not what they expected.

What is the morality of their act? Was it person-centered? Were
they acting responsibly toward one another and others? Are they
morally responsible for the exhibitionism, which they subsequently
regretted? To what extent were they realizing or exploiting their
sexuality in this experiment? What is the morality of experimentation
and acting out of curiosity in sex? Can it be determined apart from
foreseeable consequences in a particular situation? What were Mary
and her husband saying about their sexuality and their sex life when
they decided to experiment? Many of these questions can only be
answered by Mary and her husband. But they are the kind of questions which the use of drugs in relation to sex raises for the new
moralist.

postscript:
toward an
uncertain future

IT IS DIFFICULT to draw concrete conclusions from the kind of discussion which has occupied the preceding chapters. This is partly because we have been drawing conclusions along the way regarding the complexity of all sexual behavior. It is partly because sexuality itself remains essentially mysterious. And it is partly because our moral perspective will not tolerate definitive conclusions about any particular form of sexual expression. Without looking at decisions in their situation we cannot theorize about their meaning or their morality. And we can never generalize on our theories.

Consequently, no reader should close the covers of this book persuaded that certain things are always right and others always wrong in the realm of sexual behavior. But I hope there has been persuasion here, because that has been my purpose.

I hope there has been confrontation with the complexity of meanings and motives in sexual behavior. If so, that confrontation might make us more cautious in judging others, more stringent in examining ourselves.

I hope too that a Christian understanding of sex and marriage has been clarified. If so, this might be used for self-criticism of our sexual behavior, married or unmarried. It might also make us more appreciative of the dimension of interpersonal commitment which can attach to human sexuality.

I hope there has also been some insight into the mystery and power of sexuality itself. This includes the ways in which sex is basic to our sense of who we are and to some of our most fundamental attitudes. In light of this, perhaps we can stand with more genuine awe in the face of our sexuality and at the same time be more realistic in making decisions about it. We can refuse to trivialize sex through either legalism or hedonism. And we can refuse to worship sex through either superstition or commercialization.

Finally, I hope that the reader has also found instruction here in the fundamentals of Christian morality. Appreciation of the basic person-centeredness of a Christian/humanist ethic might provoke us to ask more contextual questions before passing moral judgments on ourselves or others.

Therefore, this book must end, not with conclusions, but with open-ended questions and challenges. That is characteristic of the new morality. It means that the *uncertain future* of myriad sexual decisions is in the hands of the individual moral agent, in this case the reader. I have no greater hope than that he may continue to apply the eternal ideal of being-for-others amidst the flux of social change and in ever new contexts.

notes

INTRODUCTION

1. In a generally helpful and informative book on this subject, Richard F. Hettlinger has nonetheless aggravated this error with a catchy, but misleading title: *Living with Sex: The Student's Dilemma* (New York: The Seabury Press, 1966). The fact is that "living with sex" is everyone's dilemma, as Hettlinger makes clear in his discussion of the moral hypocrisy of parents which has compounded the contemporary student's dilemma.

2. Highly recommended are two recent studies from quite different quarters. William H. Masters, M.D., and Virginia E. Johnson, *Human Sexual Response* (Boston: Little, Brown & Co., 1966) is a careful and bold piece of research into the physiological/psychological dimensions of sexual practices in our time, including factors which tend to inhibit sexual fulfillment. John F. Cuber and Peggy B. Harroff, *The Significant Americans* (New York: Appleton-Century-Crofts, 1965) is essentially a sociological study which shuns statistics and utilizes depth interviews to document the confusion and hypocrisy which characterize sexual behavior among the affluent in contemporary American society.

3. See, for example, Helmut Thielicke, *The Ethics of Sex,* tr. John W. Doberstein (New York: Harper & Row, 1964); Robert Grimm, *Love and Sexuality* (New York: Association Press, 1964); J. C. Wynn, ed., *Sex, Family, and Society* (New York: Association Press, 1966); and Hettlinger, *op. cit.* As the title implies, Thielicke's work is more explicitly concerned with ethics, but his point of view is hardly that of the new morality. And in the present author's opinion he begs the big questions concerning premarital behavior. A recent and provocative contribution from a Roman Catholic viewpoint is Abel Jeanniere, *The Anthropology of Sex,* tr. Julie Kernan (New York: Harper & Row, 1967; first published 1964).

4. The best recent works are Paul Lehmann, *Ethics in a Christian Context* (New York: Harper & Row, 1963); John A. T. Robinson, *Christian Morals Today* (Philadelphia: Westminster Press, 1964); Joseph Fletcher, *Situation Ethics* (Philadelphia: Westminster Press, 1966); and Fletcher, *Moral Responsibility* (Philadelphia: Westminster Press, 1967). The latter contains the most extensive discussions of sex from a new morality perspective.

5. These emphases are central to "existential" therapy, as well as the "logotherapy" set forth by Viktor Frankl (*Man's Search for Meaning* [New York: Washington Square Press, 1959]). These essentially secular movements in the field of counseling and psychotherapy may help pastoral theology rediscover its important dimension of value and meaning.

CHAPTER 1—THE MYSTERY OF SEXUALITY

1. For a sensitive portrayal of this ambivalence, see James Michener's treatment of the life and death dimensions in the worship of the Canaanite fertility goddess Astarte in *The Source* (New York: Random House, 1965).

2. I have in mind the therapist's use of sexual guilt feelings to manipulate the behavior of his patient.

3. (New York: New American Library, 1956).

4. The philosophical and anthropological implications of this view are discussed in greater detail in David Bakan's *The Duality of Human Existence* (Chicago: Rand McNally & Co., 1966). See also Abel Jeanniere, *The Anthropology of Sex,* tr. Julie Kernan (New York: Harper & Row, 1967; first published in 1964).

5. See, for example, *The Psychopathology of Everyday Life,* in which the sexual dimension of all human relationships is detected behind apparently meaningless rituals and habits.

6. See, for example, Deut. 24:1–5; 25:5–10.

7. Gen. 1:27.

8. I John 4:16.

9. Gal. 3:28. See also Rom. 10:12; Luke 20:35.

10. See, for example, *Psyche and Symbol,* especially Ch. 1.

11. See especially Jung's introduction to *Answer to Job.*

12. The whole medieval legal system, from which the western world is just now in the process of emerging, presupposes the superiority and self-sufficiency of the male. This is particularly clear in medieval marriage rites which show a tenacious power of survival, even in the present time.

13. See, for example, *The Interpretation of Dreams.*

14. Paul, whose attitudes toward sex seem at times ambiguous, occasionally implies this heresy. See, for example, I Cor. 7:1–8.

15. The irony is compounded by the fact that traces of this heresy could appear in the thinking of Paul, whose theology is otherwise so thoroughly incarnational.

16. More fully elaborated in *Totem and Taboo,* and elsewhere.

17. See, for example, Nathan Ackerman, *The Psychodynamics of Family Life* (New York: Basic Books, 1958).

18. The most extensive discussion of the ideological differences between Freud and Jung is given by Ernest Jones in his three-volume biography of Freud (*Life and Work of Sigmund Freud* [New York: Basic Books, 1953–57]). For a perspective more sympathetic to Jung, see Ira Progoff, *The Death and Rebirth of Psychology* (New York: Julian Press, 1956).

19. This eventuality is implied in Barbara Ward's provocative essay, *The Rich Nations and the Poor Nations* (New York: W. W. Norton & Co., 1962).

20. This concept appears frequently in the writings of Kurt Goldstein and Karen Horney. For a sensitive picture of the identity crisis of modern man, see Allen Wheelis, *The Quest for Identity* (New York: W.W. Norton &

Co., 1958). An excellent clinical discussion of the same concept is given in Erik Erikson, *Identity and the Life Cycle* (New York: International Universities Press, 1959).

21. In Hebrew worship and the reading of Scripture, the name of God, *YHWH,* is never pronounced, but replaced by a surrogate, *Adonai.*

22. For example, de Orczy, *The Scarlet Pimpernel.* Shakespeare also makes good use of this literary device. See, for example, *As You Like It* and *Twelfth Night.*

23. I Cor. 6:20.

24. Paul was also speaking here of the body as a temple of the Holy Spirit, the divine love incarnate in man. But the touchstone of the spirit of Christ is always the individual human spirit which responds to the divine imperative.

25. In spite of its trivializing of sex through the "Playboy image," the magazine has made significant contributions to the current dialogue on sexual mores. And it has championed legislative reform in what are generally wholesome directions.

26. Compare, for example, I Cor. 7, in which Paul seems to trivialize sex in the light of what he interprets to be the imminence of the day of judgment, and I Cor. 6, which ends with the exhortation to "glorify God in your bodies."

CHAPTER 2—THE EXPLOITATION OF SEXUALITY: SEXUAL IMMORALITY

1. What are cited here are overt homosexual practices. This observation does not contradict the earlier point concerning the extent to which physical expressions of affection are more tolerated among women than among men. Indeed, the two attitudes are related, and meet at the point where each devalues the sexuality of woman. Overt expressions of affection are tolerated because woman is not considered as sexually charged or dangerous as man. But for the same reason, overt female homosexuality seems to many to be even more deranged than its male counterpart, although there are fewer legal sanctions against it.

2. See, for example, William H. Masters, M.D., and Virginia E. Johnson, *Human Sexual Response* (Boston: Little, Brown & Co., 1966).

3. This is also due to recognition that women "have more to lose" through an unmarried pregnancy, or due to some cultic thinking about virginity, to be discussed below. But there is still a widespread myth that it is easier for women to control aroused sexual desire.

4. The "used goods" image cited earlier is, for example, rarely applied to the sexual experimentation of the unmarried male, which is usually dismissed as the sowing of wild oats.

5. Both D. H. Lawrence and Nikos Kazantzakis offer provocative speculations on the implications of Jesus's sexuality for his true manhood, the former in *The Man Who Died* and the latter in *The Last Temptation of Christ* (New York: Simon & Schuster, 1960).

6. Luke 1:38.
7. Matt. 1:22–23; Isa. 7:14.
8. Matt. 19:12.
9. I Cor. 7:8.
10. See "Sex and Secularization" in *The Secular City* (New York: The Macmillan Co., 1965), Ch. 9.
11. For example, in *Totem and Taboo.*
12. (Philadelphia: J. B. Lippincott Co., 1960).
13. See, for example, Havelock Ellis, "Love and Pain" in *Studies in the Psychology of Sex* (New York: Random House, 1936), Vol. I, Pt. 2, pp. 66-ff.
14. Some Freudians would, of course, argue that such compulsive oral practices are themselves sublimated expressions of basic sexual needs.
15. John 10:10.

CHAPTER 3–THE REALIZATION OF SEXUALITY: SEXUAL MORALITY

1. Gal. 3:24.
2. For a clear and systematic elaboration of the Christian rationale for civil disobedience, see Martin Luther King Jr., "Letter From Birmingham Jail," *The Christian Century,* Vol. LXXX, No. 24 (June 12, 1963).
3. Soren Kierkegaard, in *Fear and Trembling,* points out that Abraham's proposed sacrifice of Isaac in response to a divine command represents a "teleological suspension of the ethical," i.e., a suspension of normal ethical considerations in the name of a higher ideal. This is why the incident can be rightly viewed as a test of Abraham's faith. Kierkegaard's phrase is a happier one than the imagery of ends justifying means, because from a biblical perspective no final distinction can be made between ends and means.

   One of the many striking similarities between Socrates and Jesus, of course, is their common loyalty to the spirit of a law which they repeatedly violated.
4. See particularly Rogers's *Client-Centered Therapy* (Boston: Houghton Mifflin Co. 1951).
5. Matt. 5:21–22.
6. Matt. 5:17.
7. Matt. 12:1–8.
8. See especially *On Becoming a Person* (Boston: Houghton Mifflin Co., 1961), pp. 119 ff.
9. II Cor. 3:3.
10. In *The Lonely Crowd* (New Haven: Yale University Press, 1958).
11. For an elaboration of this paradox of the Christian ethic, see William Stringfellow, *Free in Obedience* (New York: The Seabury Press, 1964).

12. For an elaboration of the implications of the latter concept, see "Student-Centered Teaching as Experienced by a Participant" in *On Becoming a Person, op. cit.,* Ch. 15.

13. See especially "The Man for Others" in *Honest to God* (Philadelphia: Westminster Press, 1963), Ch. 4.

14. In *I and Thou,* tr. R. Gregor Smith (New York: Charles Scribner's Sons, 1958).

15. For example, Karl Barth. See especially "The Problem of Ethics Today" in *The Word of God and the Word of Man* (Grand Rapids: Zondervan Publishing House, 1935), Ch. V.

16. See a work of the same title by Thomas a Kempis.

17. In our time, the reader may ponder how the House Committee on Un-American Activities would respond to such a blasphemer.

18. John 5:1–18; Matt 12:1–8.

19. Mark 14:3–9.

20. Rom. 8:14. See also Gal. 4:4–7.

21. Matt. 25:40.

22. Luke 10:25–37.

23. See, for example, John 10:1–17.

24. See for example, Luke 22:24–27; John 13:1–20.

25. For example, see Isaiah 42:1–4; 49:1–6; 52:13–15; 53:1–9.

26. Matt. 7:21.

27. Mark 3:27.

28. See, for example, Matt. 10:38–39.

29. Richard F. Hettlinger, *Living With Sex: The Student's Dilemma* (New York: The Seabury Press, 1966), Ch. 10.

30. See Joseph Fletcher, *Situation Ethics* (Philadelphia: Westminster Press, 1966), pp. 146 ff.

31. Interestingly, this was the view of Freud, who is so frequently made the villain in the contemporary questioning of sexual mores. For a sensitive portrayal of Freud's legalism, see Philip Rieff, *Freud: The Mind of a Moralist* (New York: Viking Press, 1959). This point of view is also clear in Freud's own *Civilization and Its Discontents.*

32. See, for example, Rom. 5–8.

33. Mark 10:5.

34. See, for example, Rom. 6:1–11.

35. This is the danger of casuistry, when it is codified, and the reason that it is eschewed by new moralists.

CHAPTER 4—SEX AND MARRIAGE

1. See, for example, Exod. 6:2 ff.; Heb. 9:15 ff.

2. This is probably due to the preservation of a more explicit patriarchal frame of reference within Judaism. The woman, reflecting biblical prac-

tice, is not deemed capable of making a covenant. It may also be related to the analogy which sees a covenanted church as the bride of Christ, although this analogy also appears in the Hebraic tradition where Israel is seen as the bride of *YHWH*.

3. Exod. 19 ff.

4. It has become popular to make a distinction between covenants of parity and covenants of suzerainty, each reflecting certain ancient near-eastern practices. The former is a contract between equals, the latter between unequals, as when a monarch covenants certain responsibilities toward his people. The biblical covenant between God and man is a covenant of suzerainty. It is given by God, who maintains his superiority even in the covenant relationship, although the covenant nonetheless requires the free assent of man. In recent times the Christian covenant understanding of marriage has been closer to the model of a covenant of parity.

5. See, for example, Jer. 11:1 ff.; 23:5 ff.; 31:31-40.

6. For example, the view popular among some college students that sexual intercourse is something a girl owes a boy after a certain number of dates is not only dehumanizing and reflective of the double standard. It also violates the criterion of mutual consent in heterosexual relations.

7. Gen. 9:8 ff.; 17:1 ff.

8. See, for example, Josh. 24; II Kings 23:1-3.

9. For example, an earlier form of the service now used in the Episcopal Church included in its vows the phrase: "With this ring I thee wed, and with my body I thee worship." That is a healthy recognition of the body-oriented dimension of the marriage covenant which explicitly includes it in the promises made. Unfortunately, it was deleted in a revision of the Prayer Book for use in the American church, and prospects for its restoration look dim at best.

10. Matt. 5:27-28.

11. The canons of the Episcopal Church governing marriage explicitly recognize this in making evidence of duress a formal impediment to any Episcopal priest solemnizing a marriage. To the author's knowledge, however, this condition is rarely invoked.

CHAPTER 5—BEYOND CONVENTIONAL HETEROSEXUALITY

1. Abel Jeanniere, *The Anthropology of Sex*, tr. Julie Kernan (New York: Harper & Row, 1967; first published in 1964), p. 143.

2. *Ibid.*

3. Richard F. Hettlinger, *Living With Sex: The Student's Dilemma* (New York: The Seabury Press, 1966), Ch. 7.

4. Gen. 38:6-11. Of course, spilling his seed upon the ground was not Onan's real sin. It was rather his refusal to obey the biblical injunction to impregnate his dead brother's wife (Deut. 25:5).

5. Edwin M. Schur raises this same moral principle in his excellent study of abortion, homosexuality, and drug addiction entitled *Crimes Without Victims* (Englewood Cliffs, N.J.: Prentice-Hall, 1965).

6. For our purposes, this definition focuses on overt behavior more than motives. I would agree, however, with Judd Marmor in his broader clinical definition of a homosexual as "one who is motivated, in adult life, by a definite preferential erotic attraction to members of the same sex, and who usually (but not necessarily) engages in overt sexual relations with them" (Judd Marmor, ed., *Sexual Inversion* [New York: Basic Books, 1965], p. 4). See also the excellent Ch. by Thomas S. Szasz, on "Legal and Moral Aspects of Homosexuality."

7. See, for example, the widely-publicized Wolfenden Report in Great Britain; *Towards a Quaker View of Sex,* produced by a group of British Friends; and most recently the Model Penal Code proposals of the American Law Institute.

8. To be consistent, those who hold this position should be as legalistic about other kinds of murder, such as organized warfare and capital punishment, but they rarely are.

9. This is proclaimed by evangelists for the drug cult such as Drs. Richard Alpert and Timothy Leary. And a commonplace testimonial of LSD users is that "a trip isn't a trip without sex."

10. See, for example, Sidney Cohen, *Drugs of Hallucination* (London: Secker and Warburg, 1965); Robert S. DeRopp, *Drugs and the Mind* (New York: Grove Press, 1960); and Peter Laurie, *Drugs* (Baltimore: Penguin Books, 1967). The brief report of the Medical Society of the County of New York, Vol. XXII, No.9 (May 5, 1966), is also informative.

11. Although it does not prove any moral point regarding drug usage, students are quick to point out the parallels between their own use of drugs and their parents' use of alcohol, particularly in relation to sexual activity.